GIVE US THIS DAY

All the authors' royalties from the sale of this book will be donated to charities involved in the care of the terminally ill and in sharing God's love with the needy.

Give Us This Day

FIONA CASTLE
WITH JAN GREENOUGH

KINGSWAY PUBLICATIONS
EASTBOURNE

First published 1993
Reprinted 1993 (three times)

ISBN 0 85476 414 3

Produced by Bookprint Creative Services
P.O. Box 827, BN23 6NX, England for
KINGSWAY PUBLICATIONS LTD
Lottbridge Drove, Eastbourne, E Sussex BN23 6NT.
Printed in England by Clays Ltd, St Ives plc

Foreword

Had anyone told me twenty years ago that I would one day write a foreword for a book written by my wife, I would have thought them totally crazy! But then, if anyone had told me twenty years ago that my relationship with Fiona would become so complete and nigh-perfect, I would have thought them equally mad.

The ups and downs of married life take an almost impossible toll on both parties, but when the calm arrives, by the wonderful grace of God, the powerful peace and understanding that result are the greatest experience one could hope for.

I hope Fiona's telling of some of our ups and downs will bring you a measure of that same peace and understanding.

Roy Castle

Chapter 1

It was the middle of the night, and through the mists of sleep I was dimly aware of Roy moving around the bedroom.

'Roy? What's the matter?'

'Nothing, darling, go back to sleep,' came the answer. I dozed again, but soon realised that he was still awake, sitting on the side of the bed.

I sat up. 'Roy, what is it? Can't you sleep?' He covered his face with his hands; when he spoke, his voice sounded muffled. 'It's my head. The pain's terrible, and it's getting worse.'

Now that I was fully awake, I remembered—he'd gone to bed early, before me. I'd been teasing him about having jet-lag, because we had just got home from a holiday in Australia, and while I had gone straight back into a routine of housework, travelling and speaking engagements, he had been complaining of tiredness and headaches. He'd even taken an aspirin!

I snapped on the bedside light. 'How about another pill?' I suggested, 'and a hot drink?' A headache didn't seem to be very serious to me.

Roy winced with pain. 'It's too bad for that; aspirin won't touch it. I think you'd better get the doctor.'

It was his asking for the doctor that convinced me—he never willingly saw a doctor, and usually shrugged off any minor ailments as unimportant. Anyway, he was hardly ever ill—he is one of the fittest people I know. I got up and put my arms around him.

'Darling, are you serious? Is it really that bad?'

'I feel terrible—I've never had a headache like this.'

'Oh, don't be silly,' I said cheerfully. 'It's probably just jet-lag. You'll feel better in the morning.'

'I think I'm going to die. I love you, Fiona,' he said. 'Don't ever forget that. I think this is it.'

Suddenly my heart seemed to be in my throat. He really did think he was dying—he was saying goodbye.

'Sit down,' I said in a strangled voice, 'while I call the doctor. I'm sure he'll be able to sort it out. Don't worry, darling.'

I dialled the doctor's number and looked at the clock as I waited for an answer. Two am. I would get through to our own practice, but not necessarily to our own GP. Sure enough, the phone was answered by the duty doctor, who was willing enough to come out and visit Roy. Would I just give her directions to get to our house?

I fought to keep my voice calm as I described the route she should take—I didn't want her getting lost on the way and wasting more precious time.

As I put the phone down I wondered what could be making Roy feel so ill. Could he be having a heart attack? I tried taking his pulse, but my own hands were shaking now, and I wasn't really very sure what I should be feeling for. I had nursed the children through their various illnesses, but my nursing skills weren't up to first aid in a major crisis. It seemed like hours before the doctor arrived, though it could only have been a few minutes. She gave Roy a thorough examination, and said that she couldn't find anything obviously wrong. His heart was all right—I'd specially asked about that—but he was still clearly in such pain that

8

she thought he ought to be admitted to hospital for observation. I didn't want to drive with him in that state, so she called an ambulance.

It's typical of Roy that when the ambulance arrived he was sitting on the side of the bed, clutching his head in his hands; yet as soon as the ambulance men came in and began tucking him into a chair to carry him outside, he started laughing and joking with them. I felt quite exasperated—surely they'd think that if he was fit enough to joke, he must be making a fuss about nothing! But as he was lifted into the ambulance I looked at his face, pinched and white with pain, and my heart lurched again. Something was badly wrong with him, and I was powerless to help.

The ambulance drove away and I rushed back into the house, scurrying around the bedroom to collect Roy's overnight things. Our daughter Antonia, who is twenty-three, came sleepily out onto the landing.

'What's going on, Mum?' she asked. 'Where's Dad?' I told her, briefly, that he'd gone into hospital with a bad headache, but that there wasn't anything to worry about.

'You go back to bed. I'll let you know when I get home again.'

Then I hurried down to the car, threw the bag into the back, and drove off after the ambulance.

That night as I drove to the hospital I had no idea what lay ahead of us in the days and weeks to come; however, I was conscious that in the months before, God had been preparing me for a time of testing by reminding of that verse in Job, 'Though he slay me, yet will I trust him' (Job 13:15).

Some six months previously I had been thanking God for all my blessings, when a strange thought came into my mind: what would I do if my wonderful life became difficult, if something awful happened? Would I still be able to trust the Lord if everything was bleak? Could God trust me

9

with the bad times as well as the good? I hoped so. I hoped my faith was not so weak as to falter at the first hurdle. Yet the thought returned again and again. It put me in mind of Simon Peter, when Jesus said to him repeatedly, 'Peter, do you love me?'

The month before Roy was taken ill, we had planned a holiday in Australia. I was not enthusiastic—it seemed such self-indulgence to leave the family to fend for themselves just after Christmas (though all four children are over eighteen!). I found it hard to do something 'just for us', and I asked God to show us if it was the right thing to do— to close the door on our plans, even right at the last minute, if they were indeed selfish ones. Yet he did not. Everything slipped smoothly into place.

We flew to Brisbane and arrived about midnight, with no plans and no reservations. I was tired, and began to think the whole trip had been a mistake. However, at the airport there was a sort of showcase of local motels, and we telephoned the nearest one, who sent a car to collect us and settled us in no time. We spent a day or so sightseeing, then flew north to Cairns, in North Queensland, where we found another magnificent hotel. It offered only bed and breakfast, but what a breakfast! Every possible kind of fruit was available whole or squeezed—from melon and passionfruit to grapes. Exotic mueslis were on offer, and also a full Japanese meal complete with raw fish. Each day we would feast on this breakfast, pass over lunch, and walk into the local Woolworths to buy cheese and celery for supper which we would eat in our room.

The weather was tropical (around 37 degrees) and we did lots of walking and sightseeing during the day. In the evenings we found we were bitten unmercifully by the insects if we ventured out, so we relaxed and read in our room. Each night we were treated to the sight of hundreds of flying foxes coming in to land in the nearby trees; the sky was black with them, and one night Roy rushed out with a video camera to capture the scene.

Most spectacular of all, though, was the Great Barrier Reef. We made trips out to it on a power boat, and went snorkelling (after some expert instruction!). It was incredible to lie in the water looking down through the clear sea at the amazing colours of the coral, the giant clams and sea anemones, and the shoals of fish flashing past just below the surface.

Above all, it was good to have time for each other; to do things together without having to plan around two busy schedules, and even those of our family. We realised that this was indeed a God-given holiday, a chance to refresh and enrich our relationship. As we lazed in the sun, we both reflected on how contented we were to be together. I had the chance to catch up on a lot of reading and study, and some thinking and prayer, too. During that time I wrote down some of my thoughts in a notebook; in particular, that my great desire was to make Roy glad that he'd married me, for the rest of our lives. It seemed rather a far-fetched idea, in a way; yet I was increasingly aware of what a faithful, wonderful husband he'd been to me for almost thirty years. Our marriage had not always run smoothly, and we had our share of difficulties and differences. I was so thankful that even before I came to know God as I do now, I had still believed firmly in the sanctity of our marriage vows and our complete fidelity to each other. In the hard times that dutiful adherence to our vows had probably kept us together; I was so glad we had weathered those times, and coming to know Jesus as my saviour transformed our marriage and my life. Even though Roy's work sometimes involved him being away from home, I always hated partings and was glad when it was time for him to return home.

As I drove through the deserted streets that fateful Saturday night, I was praying that there was nothing seriously wrong. I knew I had to entrust Roy to the doctors' care, but part of me was cold with fear at this parting which we hadn't expected.

The hospital was in High Wycombe, only about twelve miles away, so the drive took only about a quarter of an hour. I parked outside and found my way to the casualty department. Fortunately they were having a quiet night, and the ambulance men were still there, chatting to the receptionist. They directed me to Roy's cubicle, and I found him propped up in bed, wired up to some alarming-looking machines which were monitoring his heart. However, he looked ridiculously fit, tanned and healthy from the Australian sun and laughing and chatting with the nurses. I had the strange feeling that everything was unreal—it couldn't really be happening.

After a while, Roy was moved on a trolley up to the ward, and put into bed in a side ward. The nurse in charge suggested that I should go home and get some sleep, and Roy should sleep too.

By the time I got home it was about five o'clock; still dark, but I remember hearing a bird begin to sing in the garden. I didn't go back to bed—as I usually get up at about six it didn't seem worth it.

At nine o'clock the telephone rang; to my surprise it was Roy.

'Fiona? Can you come and get me, please? They're discharging me! Yes, I'm fine—well, still a bit of a headache, but nothing like it was. How soon can you get here?'

I fetched him home, he went to bed and fell asleep. I went to church and about my usual Sunday activities, looking in on him from time to time, and taking up some lunch and supper. He was reading or writing letters, and the migraine medication the hospital had given him seemed to be working. The nightmare was over—just one of those random

12

things, I thought. It probably wouldn't happen again. Maybe it was migraine after all.

However, that night the same thing happened—he woke at about 3 am in terrible pain, and paced the room holding his head. This time I was more confident, because I knew that the hospital had already checked him for epilepsy and heart trouble, so I tried to calm him down. We didn't want to bother the doctor again, after what had seemed to be a kind of 'false alarm', so we hung on until seven the next morning, when we thought that at least the doctor would have had a good night's sleep. This time our own GP came out to see him, and gave him a massive injection of migraine medication. It didn't work.

He was in pain all that day, and that night. By Tuesday afternoon he was haggard with pain and lack of sleep; he said he felt claustrophobic, as though he was encased in his own body and unable to escape. He could neither sit nor lie still, but paced up and down the room, round and round the house, endlessly, all day and all night. I was making two bridesmaid's dresses at the time, for Antonia and her friend, and the dining room was full of cut-out pieces of fabric on all the chairs, as I sat and sewed at the dining table. We have the sort of house where living-room, dining-room, hall and kitchen are all interconnected, and I remember Roy prowling round and round the circle with all the doors open, sometimes talking to me, but unable to sit still for more than a minute.

'Look, since you're so energetic, how about going out for a walk?' I suggested. We put on our coats and set off down the hill, but after about a hundred yards Roy stopped and put out a hand to steady himself.

'Let's go back home,' he said. 'I just feel so tired, I don't think I can get back up the hill.'

We turned back, and walked very slowly up the sloping drive to the house. Once indoors, he sank into an armchair as if exhausted, but almost immediately sprang up again and resumed his pacing. It was as if he was consumed by a sort of nervous energy which drained him but would not let him rest.

I tried ringing the doctor for another appointment for that evening, but no one was available until Wednesday. We passed another wakeful night.

On Wednesday morning the doctor gave Roy some very strong medication, warning him that he should not take another dose until the evening. By lunchtime, however, things had got so bad that I rang the doctor's secretary and told her that Roy was in such agony that he could not possibly wait that long for another pill. When the doctor rang us back, it was to say that he had contacted a neurologist who happened to be in the area that evening; this man would see Roy that evening at a local private hospital.

The Nuffield Hospital at Wexham was only about ten minutes away from home. The neurologist was rather late in arriving, and we were sent to a general waiting area. I was embarrassed by Roy's continual pacing—even here he could not bear to sit still. When at last the doctor arrived, I went into the consultation with Roy, as by now he was scarcely able to talk coherently. While he was getting undressed for a thorough examination, I followed the doctor out into the corridor. My father was a GP, so I have always been very aware of the importance of patients and their relations not 'making a fuss about nothing'; however, I felt I had to say something.

'Please,' I began, 'is there anything you can do? I can't begin to tell you what agony he's been in for the last four days. He did say that if you just sent him home again, he wouldn't make it.'

The consultant smiled reassuringly. 'Don't worry, Mrs Castle, I'm fixing up a bed for him here. We'll try to sort things out. Would you like to go and fetch his bag?'

Roy spent a week in the Nuffield Hospital. I visited him every day for some hours in the afternoon, and again in the evening if no friends were there. In fact he slept a lot of the time, partly because of the painkilling drugs he was taking. Although he was able to think clearly when he was awake, his speech sounded oddly slurred, as though he had been drinking. Every possible test was run—X-rays, blood tests, a lumbar puncture and a brain scan.

On the fourth evening, Roy had some good news.

'Guess what!' he said cheerfully. 'They think they've found something positive. The last set of blood tests showed that I haven't got enough sodium in my blood.'

'What on earth does that mean?' I asked. 'I didn't know you were supposed to have any!'

'No, well, neither did I. But I got the doctor to explain it. Apparently all the substances in blood have to be there in very precise proportions. If you get too little or too much— wham, you feel ill. I've got too little sodium—salt to you and me—and that controls how much water is in the blood. Too much water in the blood upsets the balance, and the brain doesn't like it. That's what's causing the headaches: my brain's protesting!'

'So can they stop the headaches?'

'They think so. It's the fluid balance in the blood that's the problem; it may mean a special diet, and restricting fluids, that's all.'

I was delighted. Something that could be corrected just by a diet didn't sound too bad. 'So when can you come home?'

'It shouldn't be long. They just want to set up the diet and check that it works for a couple of days.'

'Great. Maybe it's just a virus or an allergy or something that's caused it,' I mused.

Roy looked thoughtful. 'Yes, I said the same thing. They just said they didn't know the answer to that one yet.'

On Thursday, eight days after his admission, Roy came home and went back to work. He felt rather defeated because for the first time in his entire career he had had to cancel a show. He was very anxious to get back to normal. The headaches had cleared up with the restricted fluid diet, though he was armed with a battery of painkillers, just in case. His schedule was just as busy as ever: the Big Band Show he was hosting for BBC Radio involved lots of travelling to different venues. He had work lined up in various nightclubs and cabarets, and he was a popular choice of entertainer at functions for business conventions at London hotels. He was also planning a trip to the USA for Anglia Television in the spring, to make a series of religious programmes in which he would be travelling around looking at Christianity at work in various places—among the homeless in New York, Gospel singers in New Orleans, etc. He spent a lot of time with the producer, deciding on the content of the programmes and working out the itinerary.

In the middle of all this, the hospital suggested that he give up the low fluid diet as an experiment, since he seemed to be so stable. The monitoring showed that the condition of his blood relapsed immediately, and he was called to St Mary's, Paddington, for a morning of tests.

I still wasn't particularly concerned. I was convinced that the strange sodium loss was due to something everyday, like a virus or an allergy, and that it would eventually clear up. Roy submitted to some X-rays and a scan, came home and got on with some work.

The next morning the telephone rang at 7.30. It was the specialist at St Mary's, asking Roy to go back immediately to repeat the X-rays, as they were not happy with them. I tried to carry on with my day as usual, but this time I was beginning to question: could it possibly be something serious? Why else would they call back so early, insisting that Roy must repeat the test that day? I was glad when Roy got home at lunch time, and I could ask him what happened.

'Nothing much,' he told me. 'They just did the X-rays again. The only thing was—while they were looking at the results, one of the doctors asked me if I smoked. I said no, but I've worked a lot in smoky atmospheres. You know what they're thinking...'

I was dumbfounded. 'It can't be! You've never smoked in your life! It can't be—lung cancer. Can it?'

I'd said the word. For the first time I realised why the word 'cancer' is so avoided, why so many people try not to think about it, refuse to say it. As a clinical condition it is an illness like any other. As something that may possibly attack someone you love, it suddenly seemed like a nightmare.

After that, once the possibility had been voiced, time seemed to stand still. On one level life went on as normal; I cleaned the house, visited friends, helped at church, cooked meals and ate them. On another level, at the back of my mind there was a continual debate. Roy can't have cancer. He's never smoked in his life. But passive smoking is supposed to be almost as bad. All those nights in smoky nightclubs. But surely he couldn't play a trumpet the way he does if there was something wrong with his lungs? He can't have cancer....

A bronchoscopy was arranged for Sunday, and I drove Roy to the Nuffield Hospital after lunch (which he wasn't allowed to eat) and collected him that evening. The operation involved passing a small tube down into the lung and removing a piece of tissue for testing. The patient has to be heavily sedated, though not completely anaesthetised, and Roy could remember nothing of the ordeal.

'You were great,' said one of the doctors as we were leaving. 'You were telling us jokes the whole time!'

'You might have written them down, then,' retorted Roy.

'They might have been new material, I could use them again!'

The results were due on Tuesday.

Roy was working at home, finalising the plans for his trip to America: he was due to leave the following Sunday.

In some ways that Tuesday was the most difficult of all for me. I had hoped that the call would come early in the morning, but nothing happened. It was my day for helping with the creche at church, while a meeting was going on. Usually I like to have a cup of tea as soon as I arrive, but that day I could not swallow anything; I felt as though there was a lump in my throat. However, we had a job to do and I didn't want to disrupt the routine, so I didn't tell anyone what was going on. I had to be my normal bright, cheerful self—though inside I felt completely numb. I wasn't worrying; I just felt as though I was suspended in time, waiting endlessly to be told the news I was dreading.

That afternoon the specialist rang through to Roy, and asked him to go up to the Nuffield to see him. He refused to discuss the test results over the phone, but when Roy said, 'What about my trip to America?', he replied, 'I don't think you'll be going to America.'

I suppose we knew then, really, that the news was going to be bad, but we still had more time to get through, more waiting to do.

Roy wanted to go alone to the hospital, and in any case we were expecting a friend, Dave Foster, so I had to stay at home. Roy had recently done the voice-over for a video Dave was making for Eurovangelism in Albania; for some technical reason the sound and the pictures didn't match up properly, so the whole thing had to be done again, and the only possible time it could be done was that very evening, as Dave was flying to Moscow the next morning.

When Dave arrived Roy was still out, so I explained where he was. Dave looked shocked and offered to leave, but I knew that Roy would want to keep his promise to finish the job. We waited together, hardly speaking, till we heard the front door open and Roy came in.

We both jumped up as he came into the room.

'What's the news?' I asked. Even if one part of me had been hoping that it was all a terrible mistake, one look at Roy's face told me the truth.

'It's the worst possible,' he said quietly. 'It's the fastest-growing cancer there is. I have six months without treatment; maybe twelve months with treatment.'

There was nothing we could do, nothing we could say. Poor Dave was compelled to be in on this trauma; he could see that we needed to be alone, to try to come to terms with the most devastating situation we had ever faced, yet here was Roy resolutely keeping the lid on his emotions, and setting off in the most businesslike way to get his script. They shut themselves in the dining room to work, and I went to the kitchen to answer any phone calls so that the bell would not disturb them.

I had known it was coming, this news, ever since that first hint from the X-rays, yet now it was certain I felt deadened with the shock. My body felt heavy, cold and numb, and I leaned against the radiator for warmth. My thoughts went round and round in circles, until I reached out instinctively in prayer.

'Lord, what's going on? Why is this happening? What are you doing to us? What's the purpose of all this? What are you telling us through this?' The questions went on and on, not making much sense, but reaching out to the Father whom I loved and trusted, and who I knew had the power to bring us through. I didn't feel angry with God, and I didn't feel that it was a burden he had designed and placed upon us; I just felt weak with shock, and held out my hands for the reassurance of his love.

I stood there shivering a while, but soon I began to feel relaxed and calm. I began to feel the reassurance I'd been longing for, and I knew that I would eventually have peace—though whether through Roy's healing, or through his death, I had no idea.

It seemed a very long time before Roy and Dave finished their work in the dining room, and then we had to watch the whole video through to check it. Afterwards Dave escaped as fast as he could.

When we were alone at last, we held each other tightly and burst into tears. We faced the truth together and wept, letting go all the dreadful tension of the last weeks. We knew that there were worse times ahead of us, but in the shadow of sudden illness, you realise just how precious every moment together really is. Suddenly the prayer I had prayed on holiday—'Lord, let me make Roy glad he married me, for the rest of our lives'—seemed unbearably poignant. How long, in fact, would we have?

Chapter 2

When this crisis descended upon us, Roy and I had a great deal to look back on with thankfulness. We had been married for nearly thirty years, had brought up four children, and had weathered all the various storms that any marriage brings. In addition, we had coped with the extra strains of being a 'show business' family—the long separations, the press attention, and the necessity to present a 'public' face to the world. Fortunately this was not an alien world to me; before our marriage I, too, had been on the stage in London, so I was familiar with the rather eccentric lifestyle which comes with a performer's career.

I was born in West Kirby, a small seaside town in Merseyside, in 1940. My father was a hard-working local GP, one of 'the old school'—always polite, long-suffering, and like many doctors at that time, on duty twenty-four hours a day. If he ever wanted a day off, he had to go out of town, or else he would surely be called out to visit someone. He was loved and respected by his family, patients and friends for his compassion, common sense and self-discipline—qualities he instilled in his children, too.

My mother was trained as a teacher of PE and ballroom dancing, but gave up her career when she married. But that certainly didn't mean that she stopped working! As well as running the house and caring for us she acted as secretary and receptionist for my father, often giving up a lot of time to comfort worried parents and relatives of patients, and visiting the sick and bereaved. She also cleaned three surgeries every day before breakfast.

Ours was a busy household; as well as her own four children, Mum also found herself looking after an extended family of various servicemen during and after the war. Some of them — Poles, Australians and Canadians — were effectively displaced persons on their way into or out of the services, and mostly they had no ration books and no homes. Our sitting room was always like a dormitory, with mattresses all over the floor, and Mum worked miracles in eking out our meagre rations to feed the extra mouths. She darned their socks, listened to their life stories, and found ways to help them contact their own families; all this while giving practical support to my father's work.

All this seemed perfectly normal to me, born during the war. I had never known anything but rationing, and I grew up in a house where there was always something going on! My brother Tony was thirteen years old when I was born; he joined the Navy before the end of the war, and later became an engineer, working his way up from the shop floor in a factory in Birkenhead. My sister Liza was eleven; she later went to art school in Liverpool and became a dress designer for Horrockses. Mauny (Maureen) was ten; she later became a secretary at the Liverpool Philharmonic. So by the time I was nine, Mauny was the only other child of the family still living at home, because she was working locally. And it was when I was nine that my life took a very decisive course.

I was happily going to the local primary school, where my favourite activity was ballet, taught by Betty Hassell of the Hammond School of Dancing. She decided that I had talent which could be fostered only by attendance at a full-time dancing school, and told my mother so. They considered various options, and finally decided on Elmhurst in Surrey—two hundred miles away! So in the summer term of 1949, when I was nine and a half years old, I was dressed in my grey and blue uniform, and went off to boarding school for the first time.

The routine at Elmhurst was incredibly disciplined; as well as our academic work and our dance classes, we were also expected to sweep the studios, serve at tables and wash up after meals. As food was still rationed the meals were very basic, and we were always hungry. At tea there was bread with a thin scrape of jam (no butter); when we were responsible for preparing the food we would spread some slices more thickly and hide them on the piled plate, where we knew we could retrieve them later! Some of the boarding houses were almost a mile away from the main school where we ate—as we walked in a crocodile through the town on our way to breakfast, we would pick up sweet chestnuts from under the trees and eat them.

I was happy enough for the first year, but succumbed to a wave of dreadful homesickness at the beginning of the second. I wrote pathetic letters home to my mother, begging her to come and take me home, and waited eagerly for her to arrive. Meanwhile, however, my mother had consulted the headmistress, who advised her to ignore me! So she wrote brief and cheerful replies, never referring to my complaints. For a while I was dreadfully miserable, but eventually realised that nothing was going to come of my pleadings, so I might as well settle down and get on with life. It was a good example of my mother's firm belief in self-discipline and common sense: she forced us to make our own way and stick to the course we were committed to.

A similar struggle took place over the academic work: some students were enjoying five or six hours' dancing a day, with the minimum of lessons. My parents decided that I must make an attempt at O levels, which restricted my dancing to one class a day, with the rest of the time being spent studying. In retrospect I appreciate their insistence; though I was never destined to be brilliant academically, it was another lesson in sticking to a task whether or not I was enjoying it, and learning the discipline of working towards a goal.

After O levels some of my friends left school, but I returned for a further year, this time to concentrate entirely on what the school taught best: dance, drama and stage-craft. Oh, the joy and freedom of being allowed to dance after all; to work towards the career in show business I longed for. I had a very happy time, especially at the end of the autumn term when I was released from school for four weeks to join a repertory company in pantomime at Worth-ing.

Cinderella at the Connaught Theatre was perhaps not the most glamorous of productions—though in retrospect I can see that it had some formidable talent in its cast, including Michael Bryant as the back end of a horse, Ted Rogers as Buttons, and Ian Holm as a poodle! My contri-bution, singing and dancing in the chorus, was not a large one, but my parents came to see me. The first night was on Christmas Eve, and afterwards we went back to the rather shabby hotel I had booked them into. It was when I saw my father resignedly playing party games in the lounge with the other residents that I realised that he really wasn't enjoying the experience at all. I remembered family outings to pantomimes when I was a child: as we watched the dancers in their sparkling costumes leaping across the stage, he would say to me, 'Do you *really* want to do that for a living?' and sigh as I always replied, 'Yes, I want to do that more than anything else in the world!'

Now I realised that all along he had merely been waiting for me to grow out of this particular fad; he had hoped that this experience of being on the stage for the first time would get it out of my system once and for all. He was wrong, of course—I was hooked, utterly and completely; I was spell-

bound by the lights, the music, the applause, by the friend-
liness of the other actors and dancers, by the sense of shared
purpose and excitement as the show came together, by the
contrast between the grubby backstage world with the
magic conjured up on stage. I had arrived!

The spring term was not too much of an anticlimax after
the excitement of Christmas, because now I had a far better
idea of just how much I still needed to learn. High-kicking
routines and tap dancing were a necessity in variety shows
in the late 1950s, and in those days a dancer's life largely
revolved around two periods: pantomime at Christmas and
summer seasons in the holiday resorts. The trick was to
secure a part in those productions which had the best
reputations (and thus made the most money) and which
ran for the longest seasons. That way you could put some
money by for the inevitable periods when you were 'resting'
(ie out of work).

That summer I spent at the Pavilion Theatre in Bournemouth, doing more chorus dancing, and returned to school
for one final term, when I was lucky enough to get a place
in the chorus in Puss in Boots at the Coventry Hippodrome.
This was a real challenge for several reasons: it included
some big stars such as Harry Secombe and Morecambe and
Wise; it was produced by Pauline Grant, who set very high
standards indeed, and we all had to work very hard; and
since (in the impenetrable logic of pantomime) it was set in
Spain, it included some Spanish flamenco dancing, and I
had to learn to play the castanets. Nowadays as my very
musical family all play their instruments all over the house,
I often bewail the fact that the only instrument I ever
learned is the castanets, and no one has ever asked me to
play them since! Coventry was one of those coveted productions with a long run—thirteen weeks—and I was paid the
princely sum of £7 10s a week.

At last I was tasting real freedom—I was earning my
own living by doing the thing I loved to do most of all; the

best kind of independence. I hadn't been let loose on the world entirely alone, however; the chaplain of Elmhurst School had arranged lodgings for three of us with a married couple who were friends of his, so we were fairly strictly chaperoned, much to my parents' relief.

In fact, the world of show business which I was entering was by no means the wild and unstructured lifestyle that perhaps they had feared. Quite apart from the supportive hand of the school chaplain as I started out, my outlook was still very much governed by my religion.

As a child I was taken to church every Sunday, though I sometimes think the most useful thing I learned was how to sit still for an hour. The emphasis of the teaching was that Jesus was a 'pattern' for us, and I can still recall deciding that I would have to try to be as good as Jesus. My resolve lasted one day—even in my innocent, childish world the going was too tough—and I realised that I couldn't manage to be entirely good purely by my own devices!

The religious life at Elmhurst was very strong, and the beautiful chapel played a central role in our lives. The flavour was 'high' Church of England, with all the ritual that implies. As little girls we were taught to be 'boat boys', carrying the incense for the thurifer—the big girl who was swinging the incense. We then progressed to being acolytes, carrying candles in their long wooden holders, and then to servers. You could only become a thurifer if you were tall enough and strong enough to get a good swing with the incense! Good voices were quickly swooped upon for the choir, so pretty well everybody was involved in one way or another. To this day the smell of incense reminds me of the smell of boiled cabbage—and the smell of boiled cabbage recalls the smell of incense—because the mixture wafting from chapel and the school kitchens characterised our Sunday mornings at Elmhurst!

Night and morning a prayer bell sounded, when we were

supposed to stop whatever we were doing and drop to our knees for prayer until a second bell released us, about three minutes later. There was a daily morning service in chapel, communion three times a week, and on Sundays we went to both morning and evening services. Understandably, one of my goals was to be confirmed and take a full part in the church's life, and so I was prepared and confirmed when I was twelve. I took this as seriously as I could, within the limits of my understanding, but I had no real concept of the mysterious Holy Spirit. Our school religious teaching was based mainly on the church's year and the meaning of the services, rather than on knowledge of the Bible, though we did study the Gospel of Mark for O level. So most of my understanding of Christianity centred around the ceremonies of the church services, rather than the everyday reality of knowing Jesus as a saviour and friend. In some ways this hampered me throughout the subsequent years, as I went on dutifully seeking God through attendance at church and my own efforts to be 'good enough'.

Because church was so important to me, I always made great efforts to attend on Sundays, wherever I happened to be working—unless I was touring, in which case most of Sunday always seemed to be taken up with standing on Crewe station! I realise now how powerful are the standards we set our children: because my parents and my school had both insisted on the importance of attendance at church, I struggled dutifully with a discipline I imposed upon myself, and suffered dreadful guilt if I failed, coupled with concern at what my parents would say if they found out! My parents certainly pointed me in the right direction spiritually and morally, and as I was not by nature a rebellious person, I did my best to follow their example. But in the matter of faith we each have to discover the reality for ourselves, and a 'handed-down' faith will not work. I'm afraid it took me a long time, with many heartaches along the way, to discover the living reality for myself.

Once I had left school and was 'resting' between shows, I went back to live with my parents. By this time my father had retired from general practice and they had moved to a cottage in the Chilterns—my father kept his hand in with medicine by doing locum work in the area. He was delighted to find that his reputation among his colleagues was such that he could easily have worked fifty-two weeks a year.

I occupied my time by travelling up to London for ballet classes to keep my dancing up to scratch, and to audition for every opening that came along. I spent a rather depressing summer in Morecambe, doing a variety show that had some famous names in its cast—Alma Cogan, Morecambe and Wise, Semprini—but which was poorly produced as far as the dancing was concerned. I was beginning to tire of my position in the chorus, where the work was rather monotonous, to say the least, and I needed more of a challenge. That autumn I came to a momentous decision. I would give myself a time-limit—say, until the next Christmas season—and if I couldn't manage to secure a decent part for myself in a Christmas production, I would give up show business and do something 'sensible'.

Fortunately for me, a series of opportunities made that Christmas a very special one. To begin with, the Royal Shakespeare Company had arranged their first-ever tour in Russia. This left the Royal Shakespeare Theatre in Stratford-upon-Avon empty, and unbelievably, someone decided to stage Mother Goose in it that year. I don't believe that such a production had ever taken place there before (or since). Certainly Billy Dainty and Ethel Revenal had never performed there before—and I had managed to get the part of Principal Girl! It was a marvellous experience to be working in that famous theatre—even in pantomime—and I took advantage of the situation by doing some work with one of the Shakespearean coaches for the company. I don't know that the lessons did much to improve the pantomime, but they were an eye-opening experience for me!

Everything seemed to work out well that year: my dressing-room (which was usually a ghastly subterranean cupboard) was a spacious room with a balcony overlooking the river; my lodgings (which had been in the past variable, to say the least) were idyllic. Of course all the homes usually occupied by the members of the RSC were available; with my 'dramatically' improved income I was able to rent a lovely flat with oak beams, belonging to Julian Glover.

That role led to a summer season of a different kind, in a small production which really smacked of the Good Companions. I was booked as the soubrette, which meant that I had to dance, sing, and be prepared to perform in sketches with the comedians. We had five different shows which we performed in rotation, changing twice weekly, in order to inveigle as many holidaymakers as possible to visit the theatre as many times as possible! It was very hard work but excellent experience. I had to learn to cope with emergencies, be amazingly versatile, and to get on with all sorts of people to keep the show running smoothly.

By this time I was becoming more established, and though there was always the inevitable autumn panic about work, I was becoming more confident that the next job really would appear from somewhere. So I left home and set up in a flat in London with an old school friend, Louanne Richards, who was working with the Royal Ballet Company. It was easier to get to my work in pantomime that Christmas in Richmond, which was at least a bit closer to the West End.

At last I was really independent of my parents, and I was determined to enjoy it. Our flat was at the top of a tall Victorian house, and completely unfurnished—so we slept on mattresses on the floor until Louanne's mother came to the rescue with some furniture she no longer needed. Louanne, like most serious ballet dancers, was incredibly disciplined, and she spent long hours training and rehearsing. My lifestyle was considerably more erratic, as I spent long periods out of work, so I took over most of the housework and cooking, which I found I enjoyed. I was mostly on the dole, so our budget was very tight, and planning food for the week was quite a challenge. When we were feeling wealthy we would buy a pound of scrag end of mutton from the local butcher, who was always very generous to us. Then we would wander down to Berwick market in the early evening, picking up bargain offers on vegetables for a stew, and smiling sweetly at the barrow boys in the hope of a few extra goodies thrown into our bags.

I don't know whether it was my mother's early training, or a gift I inherited, but I became really good at spinning out our little store of money to feed us well (dancers have good appetites!) and still have something over for our favourite treat: a croissant for breakfast on Saturday morning after we had done the weekend grocery shopping. We were certainly very poor, but I enjoyed struggling to make ends meet. Our little flat was always full of friends, and it was good to find that we could enjoy ourselves just by getting together, without any need for lavish entertaining.

This was really brought home to me just after my twenty-first birthday. I had been given some lovely gifts, including a tape recorder (they were still reel-to-reel in those days!) and some very special antique jewellery which had been handed down in my family. One morning I had been out to a ballet class and came up the final flight of stairs to our little flat to see that the door was slightly ajar.

'Louanne?' I called. 'Louanne, you've left the door open.'

There was no reply, and I hurried into the living room. It

was in a dreadful mess, with drawers pulled open and things spilled out onto the shabby rug. I could see at once that my new tape recorder was missing from the table, and of course all the jewellery was gone too.

When Louanne came in for lunch, I was still sitting at the table, numb with shock. It was a horrible feeling, having our cosy little home ransacked and our belongings turned over by the thief. We called the police, who were sympathetic, but unable to be of much help. They pointed out that our flat was at the top of a converted house, and did not even have its own proper front door. Anyone could be let in by any of the other tenants—and indeed, after some time it began to look as though the burglar had been let in by a cleaner employed in another flat. It was unlikely that any of our property would be recovered.

That was when I first began to realise the futility of setting great store on possessions. We had a great life in our little flat, with just enough money to live on, our health and our energy and the delight we had in our jobs, and lots of good friends. None of those things had been taken away from us. I decided that there was no point in grieving over mere 'things', and that even if I ever had the money, I would never want to own expensive furs or jewels.

It was that winter, while I was playing Principal Girl at the Theatre Royal, Windsor, that I had the opportunity of an audition for the part of Liesl in *The Sound of Music*. I thought I had a good chance of getting it, but I was beaten by Barbara Brown, a talented and pretty girl with considerable experience in both theatre and television. I was disappointed, but I accepted the alternative of being Barbara's understudy. At least I would be based in London, which was the best place to be for studying both singing and ballet, and also for further auditions. It also meant that I had a steady income to pay for my lessons, which were too expensive on a budget based on dole money.

31

At last I was involved in a West End production. True, it was hammered at first by the critics, who predicted that it would close after a few weeks, but it proved them all wrong for nearly five years! I stayed for two years, taking over the part of Liesl when Barbara left to have a baby, and before that filling in as one of the nuns or in other small parts. On one memorable occasion I was relaxing in the dressing room with the other 'nuns' when a frantic call over the tannoy informed me that poor Barbara had fainted on stage, and I would have to take over! Everyone rushed to help me, as I had no make-up on (the nuns were not thought to need it), and the costume I needed was still being worn by the wilting figure in the wings. I stripped off my habit and ran, listening to the dialogue on stage and trying to gauge how much time I had. Fortunately the audience were unaware that there was a half-naked under-study in the wings, desperately trying to coax a dress off a limp body and on to her own. I was supposed to climb through a window onto the stage, looking slightly dishevelled—when 'Maria' turned round to look at me, she was amazed at the reality of my performance!

It was a good feeling to be part of such a big production, and especially to be no longer at the mercy of the short runs of pantomime and summer seasons. To be employed for two years continuously is something of a dancer's dream! But I suppose I did miss the constant change of venue, and the new faces each year. During my time in variety shows I had made many good friends, as we met and moved on and met again in later productions, such as Harry Secombe and Eric Morecambe and his wife and family. One weekend when I was staying with the Morecambes, we were watching TV in the evening when Roy Castle appeared on the screen. I'd seen Roy at the London Palladium shortly after his success at the Royal Variety Performance, and thought he was a brilliant entertainer.

'Have you ever worked with Roy Castle, Eric?' I asked casually.

'Once or twice,' replied Eric. 'Good, isn't he?'

'Mmm. If you get the chance, would you introduce me?'

'Course I will,' said Eric, and nothing more was said. I assumed that he would forget all about it, but about a year later I got a phone call from Eric, saying that he was doing a TV show at the Wood Green Empire with Roy, and suggesting that I went to the show with his wife, Joan.

I arrived in a state of great excitement, looking forward to the show—until Eric dropped a bombshell. He took me round to Roy's dressing room before the show, and put his head round the door.

'Roy,' he said, 'this is Fiona and she's in love with you,' and promptly left! I could cheerfully have strangled Eric, who didn't care in the least that he had left me blushing and desperately embarrassed, trying to gather my wits to start a conversation.

As it happened, Roy was as shy as I was, and when we went out after the show for a meal with Eric and Ernie, Joan, Dickie Valentine and the whole of Chris Barber's Jazz Band, we didn't do very much talking. I must admit that I spent the next few days in a state of great expectation, hoping that Roy would ring or write, but nothing came. I resigned myself to the fact that the great romance I'd been imagining just wasn't going to happen. However, Eric, apart from being a very staunch friend, was not a man to give up easily. Morecambe and Wise were working at the London Palladium for the season; Roy had gone round to see them during the show, and Eric overheard Ernie and his wife Doreen invite Roy out to dinner after the show— 'with your girlfriend, of course.'

Roy looked embarrassed. 'Er—I haven't got a girlfriend,' he confessed.

Eric was delighted. 'No trouble,' he said. 'We'll fix you up in no time.' He picked up the phone and dialled my number at the theatre. 'Fiona, get round here right away,' he ordered. 'Roy's taking you out!'

Once again the girls in the show came to my aid. I was wearing jeans and a tatty sweater, being prepared for nothing after the performance other than going home and putting my feet up. Five minutes later I was made up, dressed in borrowed clothes, and setting off like Cinderella to the ball, leaving others to trail home in my scruffy outfit.

We had a lovely meal in a smart restaurant—a rare treat for me—and afterwards Roy plucked up sufficient courage to ask me out himself. We seemed to be on the same wavelength from the start, though Roy later teased me about some early doubts he had.

'We went back to the flat for coffee,' he recalled, 'and when you opened the fridge door to get the milk out, I could see that there was nothing at all inside except a tiny cube of cheese. And I thought, "Oh, dear, we'll be eating out of tins with this one!" '

In spite of his doubts about my housekeeping abilities, it really was the beginning of a wonderful relationship. At first I could hardly believe it was happening to me. Roy was quite a big name by now in the entertainment world, while I was completely unknown. I found it a very strange sensation when I first saw our picture in the newspapers, as I wasn't used to publicity, but Roy took it all in his stride.

'You'll get used to it,' was all he said, 'especially once we're married.'

Chapter 3

In many ways Roy's early life could hardly have been more different from mine: he was born in the village of Holmfirth, near Huddersfield, and was brought up in Scholes, nearby. He lived in a tiny house—one room upstairs and one down—which was terraced on both sides and at the back, so there was no garden or yard to play in. Down the alley there was an outside toilet shared by four families.

Roy's mother had been one of seven children (his grandmother lived next door) and she had a very good singing voice, which she would have loved to use. However, the family was poor, and she had to go to work in the mill to help feed the other children. She resolved that when she married she would not have a big family, and Roy was an only child.

As a boy he was so very small and thin that he earned the nickname 'Sparrowlegs', and his mother arranged for him to have tap dancing lessons to strengthen his legs. In fact, he claims that the lessons also strengthened his arms, because the other boys teased him so much about his dancing that he was always getting into scraps, and he rapidly became an expert fighter. He sang regularly in church, as even as a child he had a strong voice, which later developed into a powerful tenor. At the age of eight he was doing a little song and dance act in a local children's concert party—the tap dancing lessons having paid off— and at fourteen he left school and began touring with various shows. He spent four hard years touring before being called up in 1950 for National Service in the RAF, but afterwards he went straight back into show business—as the cat in Dick Whittington, doing three shows a day and being paid £5 a week.

It was when he was doing a summer season in Blackpool that he had his first break; Jimmy James had a stooge who fell ill, and Roy stood in for him. He was so good at it, feeding Jimmy the 'straight man' lines with a brilliant sense of comic timing, that he went on to tour with him for two years. This got him onto a better circuit of shows, and for a while he became better known as a comedian, though he was really a song and dance man.

The next big break came through Dickie Valentine, who saw Roy perform and liked his vitality, his sense of fun, and his versatility. He gave him a spot on his television variety show, where Roy was noticed by Bernard Delfont himself, who was preparing the 1959 Royal Variety Performance. Roy was still relatively unknown, but of course that was the show with enormous publicity and status in the business. Roy still maintains that his success was made by Prince Philip, who laughed so loudly at one of his jokes that the audience joined in and applauded wildly. After that Roy was much in demand for TV series, pantomimes and Palladium seasons, and never looked back. I can still hardly believe that I had the courage to go out with him, when I was still being a nun in the back row six nights a week!

Roy and I were married in July 1963, on a gloriously sunny day. Harry Secombe was our best man, and although Eric Morecambe was unable to be there, he was represented by his small daughter Gail, who was one of my bridesmaids. It was a big wedding, organised with much care and love by my parents, who were rather bemused at finding themselves with such a famous son-in-law. However, I think they may have been secretly relieved that at last I was doing something so normal as getting married; I had decided to leave *The Sound of Music* so that I would be free to travel with Roy. I didn't plan to join him on the stage or have anything to do with his work: Roy had seen other entertainers who had trouble with their wives interfering in their business, disagreeing with agents and so on. So I was just going to be an ordinary wife. In effect, I was giving up my career in show business to devote myself to him.

This seemed to be the sensible thing to do, apart from the fact that he was so much more established than I was: for the whole of the last year, Roy had been commuting across the Atlantic regularly to appear in the Garry Moore show on television in America. He wrote to me every day, but we found the partings very hard to bear. At one stage we considered bringing forward the date of the wedding so that we could travel together, but I knew it would wreck my parents' carefully laid plans.

So after the wedding, we sailed off across the Atlantic to spend our honeymoon in New York and Bermuda—both places where Roy was to be working, but none the less exotic and luxurious for that, especially to me who had always lived a relatively moderate lifestyle on a very limited income! Roy was more used to it by then, but he too had spent a lot of time working his way up through the clubs and cabarets and summer seasons, so he enjoyed everything doubly—partly for its own sake, and partly through my astonished amazement at our cabin on the ship, the luxury of our hotel rooms, and the welcome we received everywhere we went.

I must admit that our honeymoon did not get off to the most auspicious start: for the first few nights, I felt queasy every time we went below deck, but fortunately I soon got used to the motion of the ship and we settled down to enjoy life on board.

We sailed into New York harbour at dawn, and it was like stepping into fairyland. We spent four days sightseeing, and staying at Roy's favourite hotel, the Berkshire. Roy was well known there, and when they found that he was bringing his bride, they treated us like royalty. The Garry Moore show, in which Roy was appearing, was sponsored by Oldsmobile, and they generously lent us a car which we used to tour New England for a week in August, staying with Garry Moore at his house in Maine and sailing in his boat with him.

Then we moved on to Bermuda where Roy was booked for three weeks at a club called The Forty Thieves, back to New York for more Garry Moore shows, and then on to California where we spent Christmas with relatives. My father had eight brothers, four of whom had emigrated to California many years before, so we had a huge family reunion there, before moving on to spend the New Year in Las Vegas. All the big hotels on The Strip had floor shows with big name guests, and Roy was a great success at the Sands Hotel. To begin with we didn't want to conform to what we considered the very outlandish lifestyle of the hotels and casinos, and we determinedly had a meal and went to bed after the show. But we kept finding that we were having breakfast in the morning with people who were still in evening dress, and about to go to bed! Most of the hotels had an evening floor show and then another lounge show which ended at about three in the morning, so after a while we gave in and kept the same hours as everyone else: Roy did his show first, then we ate and went on to a lounge show somewhere else, going to bed late and rising much later! We enjoyed our stay much more once we had relaxed a bit.

The whole of the first two years of our marriage passed in a rush. We crossed and recrossed the Atlantic as Roy had bookings in England as well as TV shows in America, and the full, busy life we led scarcely gave me a moment to reflect on the career I had given up, or to consider whether I missed the theatre. To begin with we didn't have a base in England, and stayed with one or other set of parents when we were visiting. However, eventually Roy's parents moved to a smaller house by the sea, and we took over their old house in Surrey.

Our life wasn't all luxury hotels: sometimes we were staying in grubby digs with damp beds and unwashed linen! One October Roy was playing in *The Birthday Show* at the Coventry Hippodrome, and we shared a flat with Roy's pianist, Geoff Sanders, and his wife Beryl. When we arrived we were horrified—the whole place was filthy, and we had to scrub it from top to bottom before we could unpack. Irritatingly, while we were there we had an accident: a fondue set sent to us by friends in the USA had been damaged in transit, and the first time we used it, it leaked and set fire to the dining table. We had to pay the landlord for the damage, even though we had cleaned and improved the premises. Roy's only comment was, 'What about my bit of steak?'

Two years after we married, our first baby, Daniel, was born. Roy was about to set off on the American tour of *Pickwick*, with Harry Secombe, so Daniel was christened when he was only eight days old, so that Roy could be there. Two days later Roy set off to join the rest of the company, literally leaving me holding the baby. As soon as I'd had my post-natal check at six weeks, I packed up all the baby equipment and flew to Detroit to join him. This sounds like an amazingly confident and competent thing to do—in reality I was feeling quite the opposite! I had always loved babies, and had had lots of dealings with my nephews and nieces, but somehow, confronted with being in sole charge of my own baby, I seemed to have quite lost

39

my nerve. Once I was in the States, I spent a fortune on phone calls to my doctor in England—for some reason I was convinced that no one 'over there' could give me the right advice about every little spot or fever that Daniel had! I was immensely grateful for the calm expertise of Myra Secombe, who could calm a crying baby—and his mother—in no time!

Somehow, both Daniel and I survived the upheaval and panic of those early weeks, and once we were settled in our own apartment I began to enjoy my new role as a mother. Unfortunately, *Pickwick* was not a success in the States, and the show folded after only two months, so we all trailed back to England again. For the next few months we were based in Surrey, but whenever possible we travelled with Roy to his bookings around the country, so as not to be separated for too long at a time.

Daniel became a very well-travelled baby indeed: he spent his first birthday in Hollywood, where Roy was filming a TV special of *Alice Through the Looking Glass*. This was a real treat for me as I was able to visit my father's family again; as true first-generation Americans, they were incredibly hospitable, and made sure that we saw everything worth seeing in California.

By this time I was expecting our second child, and when we returned to England we decided to look for a larger home. Since Roy never knew where he would be working next, the location didn't seem to matter much, so in the end we chose Gerrards Cross, which is convenient for motorways, airports, London and television centres, and also happened to be where my sister Liza lived. It proved to be a good choice, and we are living there still—we have made a few improvements to the house, and brought noise and chaos to a hitherto peaceful and orderly street. Roy claims that the houses around ours are always good value, because the noise of his trumpet, bagpipes, alpenhorn, etc, brings the price down. Friends were rather surprised when we chose a six-bedroomed house, but we told them cheerfully that we intended to fill it!

Julia was born in February 1967, and my parents kindly came and took over the running of the house and caring for Daniel and Roy while I was in hospital. I knew that when I returned home, life would be very different; I was determined that Daniel would not have cause to be jealous of his little sister, so I took care to give him as much time and attention as I possibly could. Fortunately Julia was a placid baby and easy to please, though I took a good deal of the credit for this myself, thinking that I was more relaxed the second time around. In fact, I was working very hard indeed at being relaxed!

We still managed to travel with Roy to many of his bookings, though it was becoming increasingly difficult with two children to cope with. They were often unsettled by the change of surroundings, and I was tired of continually packing and unpacking the vast quantities of equipment they needed. It was a constant problem to entertain them and keep them quiet so as not to disturb the other guests in the hotels, and I pushed the pram for miles in search of swings and slides and park areas in which to play football! It certainly wasn't the ideal lifestyle, but it seemed better than the alternative, which was for us to stay at home without Roy.

Then one summer we rented a little house in Bournemouth while Roy was doing a short summer season there. It was an ideal situation, close to the beach where the children could play, and with no hotel timetables or other guests to stop us doing exactly as we liked. We should have been blissfully happy. But somehow tension began to grow between us. Roy would be out all evening, but I never had a welcome for him when he got back. I was snappy and irritable, and I felt tired all the time. We stopped short of major arguments, because somehow we would always come to our senses and patch up our differences just in time.

However, I did realise that things were not right, and when we got home to Gerrards Cross I went to the doctor for help.

'I'm sorry to bother you,' I began. 'I just don't seem to be able to pull myself together. I feel so depressed and miserable all the time, and I'm beginning to take it out on the family. What can I do?'

The doctor was reassuring. 'More women than you realise suffer the same problems,' he said, 'but not many have the courage to own up to it.' He prescribed some medication which he said would help me to relax, and I went away feeling slightly better. At least I wasn't being entirely unreasonable, especially if my depression was something other people suffered too. In fact, I felt so encouraged that I never got round to taking the tablets, which was just as well because soon afterwards I realised that I was expecting our third baby. That doctor subsequently moved away, and I never had the courage to confess to anyone else what I was feeling—from then on I just endured it alone.

In fact, of course, I wasn't alone—Roy was enduring it with me, but as he was so often the focus of my irritability and unhappiness, I never thought about him as sharing in my misery. He is the most tolerant and long-suffering husband anyone could hope for, and put up with my moods and grumpiness for years. He always took the view that when I got a little older (he is seven years older than I am) I would have a more relaxed attitude to life! Unfortunately, as time went on, I grew more and more unbearable to live with.

When Antonia was born in 1969, Daniel was nearly four and Julia was two. My parents came once more to hold the fort while I was away, and found the two of them more than enough to cope with for a week. They were heard to express the view that they were getting too old for this sort of thing, and they rather hoped that this would be the last time they would be called upon! Nevertheless they continued to be a great support, and they were always concerned when they noticed how continually weary and irritable I seemed to be.

On one occasion, when Antonia was about seven months old, they encouraged me and Roy to go away for the weekend on our own. Daniel had been ill with gastro-enteritis and Antonia was sleeping erratically, so I was exceptionally grateful to be offered the chance of a break. When we returned (feeling much refreshed), they told us that everything had gone very well, though Daniel seemed to be a bit concerned about being left with them.

'What do you mean?' I asked. 'He's never minded before.'

'Well,' said my mother, 'I don't think he minded this time, really. But after we'd put him to bed on Friday he called me upstairs again. He said, "Granny, you're very old, aren't you?" So I said, yes, I am quite old, I suppose. "And when people are old, they die, don't they?" So I said, yes, sometimes they did. He thought about it for a minute or two, and then he said, "Do you think you'll last the weekend?" '

Daniel was already at nursery school, and whenever we set off on our travels with Roy, I had always taken him out of school without worrying. However, once he was legally bound to attend school I decided that our travelling days were over. In any case, taking three children around with us was altogether too daunting to contemplate. We had already decided that we would not take the route that some show business families took, and have a nanny to look after the children so that I could be with Roy. We had seen too many children growing up alienated from their parents because they were both absent for long periods. So we agreed that I would stay at home and provide a stable environment for the children while Roy was away.

In fact, stability was the last thing I provided, as I became more and more moody and unpredictable. I had

43

always enjoyed homemaking, from those first days in the flat with Louanne, and being a far less gregarious person than Roy, I preferred being at home to going out to socialise. However, once I was forced to stay at home with the children, my depressions crowded in. The house, which had once seemed such a refuge from the pressures of travelling, socialising and the intrusions of the press, came instead to feel like a prison.

Part of the problem was that I began to resent Roy's apparent freedom. The phone would ring with the offer of a job, and off he would go for weeks at a time. And somehow, things that worked perfectly all the time he was at home, suddenly seemed to break down as soon as he left! It seemed that no sooner had he left the house than the plumbing started leaking, the cooker stopped working, and all the children caught chicken pox! Of course I coped—I called the plumber and the repair man and got the children's prescriptions, but I felt constantly under pressure. Why wasn't Roy ever there when I needed him?

Another difficulty was that my own childhood had been very organised—there was always strict discipline, first at home and then at boarding school—so I ran my own home in the same way. It was very important to me that my house should always be clean and tidy, that the children should be beautifully dressed and well behaved, and that I should always look my best. My standards were much too high, and I was trapped by them. I would work all day and half the night to keep things as I thought they should be— not realising that the lovely home I thought I was making for Roy and the children was being made miserable by my obsession with perfection.

Often Roy would ring me after the show, usually from a restaurant where the cast had gone for a late meal. He would try to tell me all the news—how the show was going, which people he had gone out with, what food he had ordered—just to keep me in touch with what he was doing.

Unfortunately, it only made me bad tempered as I thought of the children's cold fish fingers I'd just finished up for my tea, and the lonely evening ahead of me, shut in with three children. Too often I would only give him a snappy reply and slam the phone down.

I was also aware that he was surrounded by glamorous eighteen-year-old dancers; and that not only was I no longer a dancer but my glamorous days (after three children) were probably over, too. So I worried about my weight, and every time I put on a pound or two I would starve myself to stay thin. I must say that Roy is the most faithful of husbands, and never gave me the slightest cause for concern—but lack of sleep and a poor diet made me increasingly run down, and logic and reason didn't come into my feelings much.

When Roy was away I kept going largely on nervous tension, not eating or sleeping properly, and of course there was an inevitable price to be paid. Roy would return, and as soon as he came through the door (probably tired from travelling, and looking forward to a loving welcome from the family he'd been missing) I would greet him with an outpouring of how awful things had been, how tired and lonely I was, and how inconsiderate he was to disturb the children when I'd just got them settled for bed! Many times, he has told me, he wished he could turn round and go straight back out again.

The depression returned, of course, far worse than ever before. At first, I didn't recognise it as an illness, and I had no idea that it was considered to be a clinical condition. I just knew that I would wake up in the morning with a black cloud hanging over me. I felt miserable, lonely and isolated; tired and yet ceaselessly energetic, as I drove myself to keep going from one task to the next. I was never hungry, so I would miss meals and then eat a handful of biscuits before bed, and wonder why I couldn't sleep. The more tired I became, the more erratic was my behaviour: I would hug the children one minute and shout at them the next, and I felt continually guilty that I wasn't being either a good mother or a good wife, yet I seemed to be powerless to break out of the pattern.

I never confided in anyone about how I was feeling, because it was very important to me that we should appear to be an idyllically happy family. I felt I had to keep up a front, the more so because Roy was well known, and I felt that much was expected of me. People assumed that life in show business was always glamorous, and whenever the press wrote about us they always spoke about 'the Castles' happy marriage'. I needed to appear to be a success, and the result was that I lived behind a mask.

This was never more apparent than when we went to church on Sundays. It was one of the things I insisted on: regular attendance at church had always been one of the fundamental rules of my childhood, and I wanted it to be the same for my children. Roy always came with us whenever he was at home, and he endured the Sunday-morning panic stoically. I would rush from bedroom to bedroom, screeching at the children, and dash to the kitchen to put the lunch in the oven.

'I don't know why you bother going to church,' Roy said to me one morning. 'By the time you get the children organised you're in such a bad temper that it can't possibly do you any good.'

He was right, of course, because I would sink into the pew exhausted, and immediately start to think about all the jobs I still had to do when we got home, to be ready for lunch with visitors. But as soon as we stepped inside the church door, the mask would be fixed in place, and the Castles would smile a peaceful Sunday smile at their tidy, well-behaved children, as though everything was well in their world.

It never occurred to me that church might be a place

where I could find the solution to my problem—for by now church had become part of the problem.

There were times, when the depression was at its worst, when I would fantasise about curling up under the bedclothes and never emerging. Roy could see that I was becoming more and more isolated, so he suggested various activities to get me out of the house: helping with the jumble sale, driving church members to hospital, sitting on committees for local charities. I took it all on, and simply added to the burdens I was already carrying. All the church activities became part of the treadmill on which I drove myself, trying to succeed as a wife, a mother, a church member; coming closer and closer to exhaustion and breakdown, behind a bright and public smile.

Roy and I had always wanted four children, but after three we felt we had our hands full enough, so it was four years before Benjamin was born. After stepping in to run the home during the birth of Antonia, my mother had said jokingly that if we had any more children, she and my father would get on a slow boat to China. When we knew that Benjamin was expected we got an old ticket from the local travel agency and made it out for my parents—'To China, one way'—and sent it to them in a formal-looking envelope. They puzzled over this for days until they realised that it was a subtle request that they should keep themselves free in October 1973 when the baby was due! They duly presented themselves and kept everything running smoothly while Benjamin was born, and for a few weeks afterwards, as I integrated the latest arrival into the general pattern of our hectic schedule.

Benjamin was a blessing in many ways: he was such a contented baby that he didn't add any extra tension to my already overloaded days, and the other children were all old enough to appreciate him without feeling particularly jealous. I loved having a tiny baby to look after again, and became happier and easier to get on with as a result. Roy, too, was delighted with our family, which now felt complete—and with the improvement in my temper.

But the improvement was short-lived. The inevitable tiredness from broken nights and the extra work-load began to build up, and within a year I was suffering worse depression than ever. One symptom was that I was quite unable to make any decisions, and about that time a dilemma presented itself. A friend of mine had an Australian au pair, and recommended another Australian student to me.

'You know, Fiona, she would be the ideal solution,' she told me. 'She's been here playing with our children and I can see she's so placid and friendly she'd be just right for you. I know you've always refused to have live-in help, but you need a break to spend more time with Roy. What about it? Shall I get her to come and see you?'

I played for time. 'Let me think about it,' I said. 'I'll have to talk to Roy.'

Roy was all in favour. 'Sounds ideal,' he said. 'You know you work too hard; it'll be good for you to have someone around the house for company, and to do some of the school runs for you. Maybe you could come on a couple of trips with me, too—it'd be just like the old days!'

'But, Roy,' I objected, 'we don't live the sort of life that anyone could easily fit into. Most husbands are coming home from work when you're just going out. The children don't think you work at all—you're still at home when they go to bed, and you're asleep when they get up in the morning! How do you think a stranger will cope with you coming home at five o'clock in the morning?'

Roy wasn't put off. 'She'll get used to it. The idea is that she fits in and helps us. As long as the children get on with her I don't think there'll be a problem.'

I couldn't let the matter rest, but raised every negative argument I could think of. In fact, I was rather afraid of anyone coming into the house and sharing our lives with us—she might find out what I was really like. I couldn't face the tension of having to keep the mask on and live up to my 'success' image all the time.

In the end Roy threw up his hands in despair. 'OK, that's enough. I've told you what I think, and I don't want to hear any more about it. You decide.'

Deciding was just what I couldn't do. I was torn between my desire to agree with Roy, and try to make our life better, and my fear of being unmasked by a stranger in our home. Roy refused to be drawn into it any further, so I was on my own. I was desperate.

The next morning I took the children to school and then settled Benjamin for a nap. I went up to the bedroom, closed the door, and sank down on my knees beside the bed.

'O God,' I prayed, 'if you're there at all, you've got to help me and you've got to help me now, because I've had it. I just can't cope any longer.' I got up then—I didn't really expect an answer. I didn't know if God cared, or if he was able to do anything to help me. Almost immediately the phone began ringing, and I picked it up wearily.

It was someone I knew only slightly, and she had a very strange request.

'Fiona,' she began, 'I don't really know why I'm phoning but I had this urge to contact you. Can we meet for coffee some time? I don't really know why, or what we'll talk about when we meet, but I just have this feeling that we need to get together.'

I recalled that Tamara was a friend of my sister's—what she called a 'committed Christian'—which in my book meant someone who had gone overboard a bit, and insisted on talking about religion all the time! In my present state I was in no mood for making dates for coffee, so I put her off.

'That would be lovely,' I lied smoothly, 'but I'm afraid I'm rather busy this week. Can we make a date for next week some time?' We consulted our diaries, made a date for the following week, and rang off.

Then I stopped and stared at the phone. A minute before I had been down on my knees, begging God for help. Here was a Christian ringing to offer me that help and I had put her off for a week! I seized the phone and tried to remember her number. I wasn't even sure of her husband's initial, and rang two or three wrong numbers before I got her again. 'Can I come round straight away, instead?' I asked. She agreed without argument.

Ben was awake now, so I picked him up, went downstairs and thrust him into Roy's arms, saying 'I'm going out'—and left. Things were so bad between us at the time that Roy thought that perhaps I really was leaving for good.

At Tamara's house I poured out all my problems, which probably didn't sound that serious to her. Rationally, I had nothing at all to be depressed about: materially I had everything I needed, I had a loving husband who provided for me and four beautiful, healthy children. What more could anyone want? It all served only to make me feel guilty about the way I was behaving. I was lonely, empty, bitter and resentful. I had everything and I had nothing. I had tried every way I knew to make life tolerable for myself and my family, and I had failed. Surely there was more to life than I had found, or what was the point in going on? If God existed and cared about us, why did he make it so hard to find him and follow him? I blurted out question after question through tears of guilt, frustration and tiredness.

Tamara listened patiently to all this and then said quietly, 'Fiona, you say that you're a Christian, that you've been going to church all your life. But have you ever actually stopped and asked Jesus to come in and take over your life?'

I was dumbfounded. 'No,' I replied, 'I didn't realise I was supposed to.' I really hadn't ever thought about it. After all, I had been christened and confirmed, went to communion regularly, and did everything I was meant to do. 'Why should I do that? Would it make any difference?'

'I think it would,' she replied gently. 'Don't you think it's about time you did it?'

'Yes, I suppose so,' I said weakly—though I think I only said it because I was afraid to say no! My back was against the wall, and I was desperate enough to try anything. Deep down I was afraid that what I was about to do would mean that I would have to try even harder, do even more, give things up and generally earn God's approval the hard way. I didn't have much faith in my ability to succeed at that. But Tamara explained to me that this wasn't about me 'doing' anything except opening my heart and letting Jesus come in. He had done the work already. By his death he had 'earned' salvation for all of us. She herself had suffered from depression for many years, so she didn't belittle my feelings and experiences, but she told me how her life had been transformed by taking this same step.

'Well,' I thought, 'at least she knows what I'm going through. If it has worked for her, maybe it will work for me.'

Tamara read me a verse from the Bible: 'Look! I have been standing at the door and I am constantly knocking. If anyone hears me calling him and opens the door, I will come in and enjoy fellowship with him and he with me' (Revelation 3:20, Living Bible). She closed her eyes and began to pray for me and with me. I had never prayed out loud without a prayer book before, and if I hadn't been crying so much I would have been embarrassed.

'Now, Fiona,' she said. 'I want you to think whether there is any area of your life which is not pleasing to God. Confess it and ask for his forgiveness.' It was a solemn moment, but I wondered fleetingly if we had enough time for all the things I needed to confess! For the first time I admitted to myself and to God the mess I had made of everything that was important to me, my family, my marriage, everything.

'Lord, please forgive me,' I prayed. 'Jesus, please come into my life and make it new.'

I realised that Jesus had been standing and knocking at the door of my heart for thirty-five years; I had never let him in, and he wouldn't force the door from his side, because he had given me free will to choose what I did with my life. As soon as I prayed that prayer, he kept his promise and came into my life, and turned it upside down. I didn't become perfect, but I knew that he had come, because I did feel the most incredible sense of peace filling my heart. It was as though someone had poured warm oil all over me, touching and soothing all the sore and hurting places in my life, and all my tensions and fears and misery drained away. I knew something real and important had happened, though I didn't fully understand how. I knew that whatever happened now, I had Jesus living in me, and I would be able to cope. Life was going to be a new adventure from now on.

Chapter 4

As I drove home that day the peace and joy I had experienced stayed with me—I even started singing in the car—and I wondered what was going to happen next. After all, I might feel the assurance that God was with me, and that I was a new person, but my circumstances were still the same. I still had the same home to run, the same family to care for and work for, the same husband with the same job. Would my feelings of peace evaporate as soon as I opened the front door?

It was only a short journey home, but during that time God showed me that I should not burst in and tell Roy what had happened. Indeed, reason told me that if I did, Roy would probably think that I'd finally flipped. My behaviour in recent weeks had been so erratic that he would have been perfectly justified in thinking that I had religious mania on top of everything, and was certifiable at last! I did notice a look of surprise and relief on his face when I went back into the house (probably because he really had been wondering if I had left him for good), but he didn't question where I had been. I realised that I had to show Roy, not just tell him what had happened—I had to let him see for himself that I really had changed. And I needed to see that for myself, too.

Roy's experience of Jesus was quite different from mine. He had been brought up to go to church regularly, and he sang in the choir in the Methodist church they attended. Church in itself he didn't find very helpful, but he seemed to grow up with a faith that grew with him. When we discussed it, much later, he put it like this: 'I always felt as though someone was holding my hand—but it was a long time before I looked up and saw who it was.'

I had grown up surrounded by the structures of a denomination, but without the reality of a relationship with God. When at last the two came together, things began to make sense. Roy, on the other hand, had slipped out of the habit of going to church fairly early, but he had never lost the reality of his relationship with God. He followed the Master in a very simple way, praying and always trusting God to show him the right thing to do.

When he met me, he was very confused by my insistence on all the rituals of the church, when it was clear that my life did not show any sign that I knew how to listen to God as he had learned to do. Before we were married I insisted that he was confirmed, and he dutifully submitted to baptism, too, since there was no record available of his baptism. Although the observation of rules was never as important to him as it was to me, he was very good-humoured about it all, and never took these things lightly.

I must admit that when I first started going out with Roy, my father described him as a 'trumped-up pop singer', but Roy's charm did its work and after a while both my father and mother adored him. The first time we went to spend the weekend with my parents I was dreading going to church on Sunday morning. As a musician, Roy was always amused by the congregation's wavering attempts at the first notes of a hymn, and he usually got the giggles. I had spoken to him very sternly about this before we set off, and he made a huge effort and preserved a suitably solemn expression. Unfortunately, half-way through the hymn a large fly alighted on my father's hymn book. Father hated flies, and started making wild attempts to slap it with his hand or even to shut it in the book. It was too much and I'm afraid we both disgraced ourselves by laughing.

We were not always treated kindly by the church. On the first occasion when the banns for our marriage were read, in the church where my mother had worshipped and worked for several years, the vicar launched into a powerful sermon violently condemning the immorality of show business. Roy and I were greatly tempted to walk out, but felt that this would embarrass my mother even more, so we sat and endured it.

After our marriage, my greatest fear was that Roy would laugh at me because I always knelt beside my bed to say my prayers at night. He never did, of course, but it is significant that I felt that my position was a vital part of the exercise. (Nowadays I pray anywhere and everywhere, without embarrassment!)

Roy was always immensely patient with my emphasis on duty—even when it disrupted our family life. Now I knew that I had to show him that things really were going to be different, without making any extravagant claims for what had happened to me. The first thing I did was to call all the committees and groups I was involved with, and tell them that for a while I would not be able to work for them. Everything from the NSPCC to the jumble sale committee would have to do without my efforts, because I had realised that I had to concentrate on my home and family.

Too often in the past I had put the children in the back of the car and told them to sit quietly and behave properly while I spent the morning ferrying people to hospital, church or library, considering my own 'righteousness' rather than the needs of my family. I would tell myself that when I had done all the 'duty' things I would have time to play with the children later, but of course by then I was so tired that I had no energy left for them, and would be more likely to snap and shout at them, or tell them to play quietly alone while I finished the housework. My church activities were leaving a trail of destruction in the family as I failed to meet the children's emotional needs, though I was punctilious in caring for their physical needs—good food, clean clothes, a tidy home.

So the first benefit was that I had more time for the family, and as the pressure of work eased, I had more energy for doing things with them. Interestingly, where I had previously felt trapped in the house, and resentful of Roy's freedom, I was now perfectly content to stay at home. It was as if I had realised the value and importance in God's eyes of the job he had given me to do, and I understood what a privilege it was to be mother to four children and a wife to Roy.

In addition, I was never again afraid when I was alone in the house at night. In the past I would lie awake for hours, listening to every creak and rustle, expecting burglars, fire, earthquake—anything! Once I rang Roy in Glasgow in the middle of the night to tell him that I could hear something tapping at the window—though what he was supposed to do about it at that distance, I can't imagine! Now I was filled with confidence and peace, as I knew that Jesus was with me all the time.

As time went on, other parts of me began to change, too. I stopped being so anxious and uptight about everything; I began to relax and enjoy life, and the dark clouds of depression lifted and vanished. One thing that improved was my ability to communicate with Roy. Before, whenever I felt depressed it was as though I pulled down a screen between us. I shut Roy out, and no matter what he did, whether he tried kindliness, sympathy, or sternness, it had no effect. Now, if I felt the cloud descending on me, I would go to him and say, 'Roy, I'm feeling ghastly,' and we would be able to talk about it. I no longer expected him to understand how I was feeling by telepathy, without being told about it, and I no longer added to my feelings of tiredness or depression by getting irritated and resentful.

It was about a month before Roy actually asked where I had been on that day, and what I had been doing. Very hesitantly, because I was still rather afraid that he would be scornful, I told him.

'I went and had coffee with Tamara and she led me to Jesus. I confessed what a mess I'd made of everything and asked him to come into my life and make it his.'

Roy's response was immediate.

'Oh, thank goodness. I've been praying for years that you'd see the light and become a reasonable human being!'

I was immensely relieved. 'I was afraid to tell you,' I confessed, 'in case you laughed at me. I'd been so awful to you that I didn't think you'd believe me if I said things were going to be different.'

'I knew straight away, when you came back that day,' said Roy. 'When you went out, everything seemed so dark and depressing, it was as if the house was all grey and grimy and covered in cobwebs. When you came back, it was as if someone had redecorated it overnight!'

'Why didn't you say anything, then?' I asked.

'Well, I was afraid it might not last. But it has, hasn't it?'

It wasn't easy, though. My outlook might have changed, but my circumstances hadn't, and becoming a Christian does not inoculate us against the trials of everyday life. Sometimes I felt as though I was tiptoeing through a minefield. If I lost my temper there was always the risk that Roy would say, 'I thought you were a Christian?' No one becomes perfect overnight, if ever, and I had to guard against many of my old habits. In particular, I was so hungry and thirsty for Christian teaching that I wanted to learn as much as I could. For a while there was a danger that I would replace my hyperactive rushing about doing good works with rushing out to meetings, and I didn't want

Roy to feel that he had an absentee wife. However, this was cleared up when we engaged the Australian girl as an au pair for three months. She proved to be a great success, and I was able to go to meetings in the mornings, when Roy was often either working or asleep.

As I absorbed more teaching from the Bible, lots of my attitudes began to change. I began to recognise the wisdom of some of the things Roy had been patiently saying to me over the years: 'You never enjoy today because you're too worried about tomorrow' ('Therefore do not worry about tomorrow, for tomorrow will worry about itself' Matthew 6:34). I stopped being so anxious about punctuality and getting everyone organised when we were going anywhere. A little while ago the children gave me a poster which illustrated this perfectly. It was a picture of hundreds of turkeys standing in a very orderly fashion, all looking up and facing the same way, and all looking absolutely identical. The caption read, 'Well, now that we're organised, what shall we do?' It was given with much love and a few giggles—I was only grateful that they were able to joke about it!

Another thing I took steps to alter was my deceitfulness. In the past I had never worried about telling the odd 'white lie' to wriggle out of something I didn't want to do, or to arrange things the way I wanted. For instance, I had always had trouble getting Antonia to go to bed earlier than the two older children (I put them to bed in order of age, very strictly, with no concessions). She would never settle down until the others were in bed, too, so I would get Daniel and Julia to pretend to go to bed with her, and whisper to them that they could come downstairs again once she was asleep. One night we heard Antonia coming downstairs again after about half an hour, and I hid the other two behind the sofa! She found them, of course, so that ploy didn't work again.

On another occasion I sent some chocolates to the

mother of one of Ben's friends, who had kindly taken him to a football match. When she rang to thank me, Ben answered the phone: 'Oh, that's all right,' I heard him saying, 'we didn't have to pay for them. They were just some old ones we had left in the cupboard from Christmas!' Meanwhile I was making frantic signals to him and blushing furiously at his honesty. The point was that for a long time I didn't automatically tell the truth, and it was a while before I understood how bad an example this was for the children, and how important it was to be honest before God.

For many years all my dealings with my children were flawed by this sort of thing. Sometimes I knew that I had treated them unfairly or shouted at them unnecessarily, but I could never bring myself to say sorry. I thought that if I apologised to them I would lose their respect, so I would twist the circumstances to justify my conduct to them and to myself. Now I realised that I could confess anything I had done wrong to God, and be free of it. I didn't have to carry around a lot of guilt all the time. Somehow this made it possible to admit when I was wrong to the children too, and say that I was sorry. To my surprise I did not lose their respect; rather, it seemed to draw us closer together, because they realised that Mum was not infallible—another release from the impossible standards I had been setting myself!

Over the months God began to put right some of the things that had been wrong in my life, and it was a joy to see how fast things improved. The children seemed more light-hearted and more secure, now that their mother was no longer snappy and unpredictable. Roy came home to a smile and a warm welcome instead of to a shrewish and tearful wife ('hatchet-faced' was how he described me!). I was feeling more in control of things than I had before;

however, the next stage for me was learning to relinquish that control of my family life.

Tamara held regular meetings in her home, sometimes just for prayer, sometimes with speakers. My faith developed very rapidly with the help of this group; I saw answers to prayer, my own struggles were supported, and I received loving teaching from the others. On one occasion Stuart Reid, then assistant pastor from Gold Hill Baptist Church, came to speak on Ephesians 5 and other texts: 'You wives must submit to your husband's leadership in the same way you submit to the Lord' (Ephesians 5:22, Living Bible). He said that the man's role was that of head of the family, and that he should make the ultimate decisions, and take responsibility for the discipline of the children.

I listened to his talk with growing impatience, and when he asked for questions afterwards, I fairly launched myself at him.

'How on earth can my husband take responsibility for the family discipline? He isn't even there most of the time! I'm the one who's on the spot and I have to deliver the discipline!'

'I'm not saying that a woman shouldn't discipline the children,' replied Stuart mildly, 'only that the big decisions about family life should be discussed between husband and wife and agreed between them. That gives security to the children because they know they can't play one off against the other.'

'And what if we can't decide?' I asked. 'What if we can't agree on the right solution?'

'Then the decision is ultimately the husband's. If it does turn out to be the wrong decision, he's far less likely to brood over it and feel guilty about it than a woman would. All she has to do is submit to his will—and remember not to say "I told you so" if it all goes wrong!'

'I'm not sure about all this,' I muttered. 'I didn't

promise to obey when I got married. I don't think all this submission thing would fit into our marriage.'

'Well,' said Stuart, 'I suggest you go home and look it all up in the Bible. That's where you'll find out God's order for the family, and if you pray about it I think you'll find that it includes you.'

I went home armed with the Bible references and looked it all up. It wasn't drudgery for me, this study of the Bible—I was really anxious to find out more of the truth, even if I didn't much like what I found.

I realised that because Roy was away so much I had been forced into being fairly independent, and running the family unaided for long periods. However, I had then taken over the whole of Roy's task as father of the family, and insisted that the children were my business, because I had the main task of looking after them. I had usurped Roy's position as head of the family, when really we should have been sharing equally the task of making decisions about discipline, so that whatever I did was the outcome of a joint decision.

I had also grown to resent the easy-going role into which I had then forced Roy; he would arrive home from lengthy trips abroad, laden with presents for the children he'd missed for so long. I would feel angry that he was seen as the warm, sunny, gift-giver, while I was saddled with being the mean mummy who was always saying 'no'. I began to understand that a great deal of imbalance in our family life stemmed from this issue of submission, and we were going to have to work through it together.

I was very keen to start putting things right at once, so that weekend I decided that I would no longer take the reins of discipline in the family, but let Roy take charge. After breakfast on Sunday I watched as the children started bickering, chasing each other round the table and knocking a pile of magazines to the floor. I waited for Roy to do his manly thing and send them all to their rooms, but he went on peacefully reading the Sunday papers as chaos reigned around him. That was when I realised that you had to be open-minded about the response; submission did not mean making your husband do what you wanted him to!

I think that on that occasion I did intervene and put a stop to the chaos, but it was clear that we needed to discuss the whole issue. It was a new idea for Roy, too; he had been happy for me to take over the discipline when he was away, though he admitted that he did sometimes think I was too strict with the children. I recall once saying to Antonia, 'Just you wait until your father gets home!'

'Oh, Dad won't smack me,' she replied airily, 'he hasn't got the courage!'

It was obvious that all the discipline needed to be agreed between us, even if I was the one who administered it. As Roy pointed out, 'I can't come in after a week away, and suddenly switch on being angry with the children for something they did last week!'

At around the same time I came across a verse in the Bible about appearances: 'Don't be concerned about the outward beauty that depends on jewellery, or beautiful clothes, or hair arrangement. Be beautiful inside, in your hearts, with the lasting charm of a gentle and a quiet spirit which is so precious to God' (1 Peter 3:3–4). I found this to be a great release for me. I always felt that I ought to look smart, and I wanted Roy to be proud of me, but this verse seemed to say that I didn't need to live up to the 'glamorous show business' image, and that as long as Roy wasn't ashamed of how I looked, then I didn't need extravagant clothes or jewels.

At last I was able to see the difference between being a Christian and merely 'going to church'. We still went to church as a family, but now I was looking for the answers to specific questions, bringing what I learned on Sunday into my life during the week. I had grasped the great good news that I didn't have to struggle to earn favour with God, because he already loved me. And I now knew that I didn't have to exhaust myself trying to be 'good' or 'righteous', because that was a lost cause: on my own I could never meet God's standards of holiness. But that didn't matter, because Jesus had died for my sins, so they were wiped out in God's eyes. All that remained for me to do was to attempt to live my life in the new way, in Jesus' way, guided by the Holy Spirit in everything I did.

Roy and I had joined a Bible study group, composed mainly of young couples from a variety of churches. Some of them came from Gold Hill Baptist Church, and they always sounded enthusiastic about the teaching they received there. I felt that I would like to hear this sort of preaching, which opened up the meaning of a Bible passage and applied it to life today. On several occasions I was tempted to go along on a Sunday evening, when my presence would not be missed at the Anglican church. Roy was away working and there was no reason why I shouldn't pay a visit to another church; on two occasions I even had my coat on, ready to go out, but at the last minute I wasn't happy about it, and stayed at home. Then one evening at the Bible study we were talking about the work of the Holy Spirit.

'Our pastor is doing a series of sermons on the Holy Spirit,' said one man. 'Why don't you come along?'

Roy was keen to go, and at last I realised what had been wrong before: I was only happy about it if Roy was there and able to take the lead. The following Sunday evening we set off for Gold Hill Baptist Church. I hadn't ever been in a Baptist church before; the strict Anglican regime in which I was brought up tended to be rather disparaging about 'chapel' as opposed to 'church'. We sneaked in at the back, feeling slightly disloyal to be even visiting a church other than our own. We both enjoyed the service, unfamiliar though it was, and we loved the teaching; it was vibrant and relevant, and seemed to speak to us in our situation, showing us the way we should be following and answering our questions. Most of all, though, we felt a great sense of love, both in the service and afterwards when we spoke to friends in the congregation. I know now that this can be found in all sorts of churches, in both the Anglican and other traditions, but at the time my experience of different churches was very limited.

Our hopes of being inconspicuous were short-lived, however. Roy is well known from his TV appearances, so there were not many people there who did not know who we were, though no one made a fuss about it. In any case, it soon became clear that even parking our car outside the Baptist church was an act guaranteed to be noticed by some of our friends. After the third person had asked casually, 'What were you doing at Gold Hill Baptist Church, then?' I realised that we were going to have to make a decision about where we went to church.

We prayed about it for a week, and asked God to show us his will in the matter. I was particularly anxious not to reject our original church, nor to flit from one church to another, and I asked God to open or close the door for us. In the end, we felt that it was wrong for us to 'sit on the fence' between the two churches, and in answer to our prayers we saw some very clear signs that God wanted us to be at Gold Hill, so we transferred our allegiance.

Interestingly, all those confirmations of the Lord's will that we received concerned the children. Later in the week, Daniel asked, 'Can I go and stay at David's overnight on Saturday?'

'Yes, of course,' I replied, but my heart sank. I had wanted us to go to the new church together as a family.

'Do you really want to go?' I asked him.

'Oh, yes,' said Daniel, 'and they'll bring me back after church.'

I thought that was the end of my plan, until he came running back into the room, to say, 'David's family go to Gold Hill Baptist Church!'

The next day I was telling a friend about my new-found faith in Jesus, when she mentioned that her daughter had been to Gold Hill. 'She'd like to go again, but she doesn't have a friend to go with,' she said. As the daughter was one of Julia's school friends, we arranged to take her with us, too.

I was worried at first about settling the children into a new Sunday school (all four in different classes in a rabbit-warren of rooms behind the church!) but they were immediately at home and very happy. They were all taught by loving, committed Christians, and in time they all came to know Jesus for themselves.

Julia was about ten when she made her commitment to Christ. She was at a convent school where one particular nun was able to show her what was meant by the gifts of the Spirit, and she began 'speaking in tongues'—praying in a new language which she had not learned—with great joy. Later on, while she was at college, her faith began to mean less to her and she went through a period of about four years while she tested everything out. Because of her ability with languages she was able to get a work placement with the European Missionary Association; she enjoyed the work, but she became increasingly impatient with what she called 'hypocritical' Christians. She was irritable in the office where her colleagues played tapes of Christian music much of the time, and she grew angry with those who persisted in smiling sweetly and seeing the good side of everything! I did not interfere, believing that all the children had to establish themselves in their own right as adults, with no intervention from me. At length she came to see that other people's hypocrisy, whether real or not, was nothing to do with her. The real issues were between her and God, and in the honesty of that encounter she came back to her faith in Jesus.

Since then I have asked her whether it would have helped if I had pursued her more during her 'down' time; she replied that if I had pushed her, it would have pushed her further away. She needed to find her own way back to the Lord, and I didn't really come into the matter.

Daniel went through a similar period of rejection when he was about sixteen, but by the time he was nineteen he, too, had found his own way back. He went to a Quaker school, which he enjoyed, but he found the quiet worship there very passive. He told me afterwards that he always felt that he was a Christian, because he had been brought up in a Christian family, but at the same time he wanted to have fun with his peer group. Gradually he stopped praying and reading the Bible, and immersed himself in the same pursuits as his friends. However, after a while he found the enjoyment he got was rather hollow, and of his own accord he came to the conclusion that either God was real, or else life was fairly pointless. He decided that he would commit his life to Jesus, since that seemed to him to be the only way to make sense of the world and find happiness.

The whole business of bringing up children can be just as difficult for a Christian parent as for the non-Christian. I was always very aware of the load of guilt I carried, because I never felt that I lived up to my parents' high standards and expectations. I have tried (and probably failed) to avoid putting pressure on the children to live up to standards imposed upon them; as Christian parents, our prayer should not be that they will succeed in life, but that they should find out God's plan for them. The best gift we can give them is to make them feel whole, accepted as the people they are.

When Antonia was about fourteen she rebelled against the high standards of cleanliness and tidiness I had set for our home. It was impossible to get her to tidy her room, and for two years we tried everything in our power to get her to conform—stopping her pocket money, curtailing outings, nagging her endlessly. In the end the issue of the tidy room was threatening to dominate our family life, when Roy took over. He decreed that we would stop nagging her about her room, but she had to take full responsibility for it—we would not go in there at all.

The relief was enormous. Suddenly we were free to discuss other things. That was when she began to talk about school—the difficulty she was having with some of her friends, whose standards were not Christian standards; the problems that arose from peer pressure and the struggles common to all teenagers. I was appalled to realise that in our obsession with one tiny aspect of her behaviour, we had failed to understand her real concerns.

I'm glad to say that we are good friends now, though her room is still untidy; Roy says that he goes in and calls to her—just in case she's there and he can't see her in the muddle!

Benjamin, our youngest child, knew that his brother and sisters were all Christians. One day when I was saying prayers with him, I told him, 'You can invite Jesus into your life and know him in a special way.'

'I know that,' he replied. 'I think I'll do it on my birthday.' He was going to be eight.

On his birthday, after the tea party and his bath, I reminded him gently of his promise.

'Well, Mum,' he yawned, 'I've had a busy day. I think I'll just do it tomorrow.' He did, too, in his matter-of-fact eight-year-old way, and has remained faithful to that commitment ever since.

All the children have found their own ways of living out their Christian faith. At the time of writing, Benjamin is still studying music in London, doing a one-year jazz course at the Guildhall, and Antonia works at the Orange

Tree Theatre in Richmond, as a stage manager. Both live at home and commute to London, and worship with us as a family on Sundays.

Julia spent some time in Peru in 1988, and has now returned there to teach English at an Adult Education Centre. Daniel has worked in Greece, Norway, Mongolia and Turkey leading missionary teams with Youth With A Mission, and is now going with his wife whom he met in Norway to Moorlands Bible College for more training.

They are all a great joy to us, especially in the faith we all share. On that day when we learned the shattering news of Roy's illness, I was so glad that we could support each other, and know that we all had the ultimate comfort of God's loving arms around us.

At the start of my stage career.

In The Sound of Music
which ran from 1961 to 1965.

Roy and I announce our engagement in January 1963.
(Photo: The Associated Press Ltd.)

Harry Secombe entertains us all at the wedding reception.

Our family is complete (1974).
(Photo: Jack Curtis).

'See how you like it!' Roy's cheerful spirit can be a hair-raising experience.

The family at Daniel's wedding in 1993.
(Left to right: Antonia, Julia, me, Birthe, Daniel, Roy, Benjamin).

Roy receives the OBE.
(Photo: The Press Association Ltd.)

Chapter 5

On that Tuesday evening, after Roy had finished working on the video and Dave had left, we sat together for a long time, trying to come to terms with what was happening. Roy had cancer. It was painful to realise that suddenly we had no future. All our immediate plans were dashed; Roy's trip to America would have to be cancelled, and everything from now on would revolve around the slim hope offered by treatment. We cried together, and talked, and cried some more. In a way I think we were both suffering from shock, even though we had been half prepared during the previous days for what the news would be.

Benjamin came home at about 10.30, took one look at our faces, and said, 'What's happened?'

'We've had the results of the tests, Benj,' said Roy gently. 'I've got cancer. They're going to start treatment straight away.'

Benjamin was silent as we explained as much as we knew about Roy's condition, looking from one to the other of us as we talked.

It was only after a while that I said, 'You know, we've all got to face this together. So it's going to be important that we're honest about our emotions—if we feel anger, or grief, or pain, we must be able to say so. It's OK to cry.' That was when Benjamin finally put his head in his hands and wept, as though I had given him permission to let his emotions out. I put my arms around him and we all cried together in a little circle.

We knew Antonia wouldn't get home until about 12.30, so we all waited up for her. She, too, realised that something was wrong as soon as she saw us all sitting round the kitchen table. When we told her she went very pale, sat down suddenly, and burst into tears. Once the first storm was over, she became angry.

'It isn't fair!' she said. 'You mustn't die, you're too young, Dad! You can't die!' She wanted to know all the details of what the doctor had said, what the prognosis was, and so on.

'The stupid thing is that I feel so well,' Roy kept saying. 'It's so hard to believe that you can have a terminal illness and feel perfectly all right.'

We went to bed at last, but I don't think any of us slept at all. I kept thinking that we'd get up in the morning and find it was all a bad dream. It was hard to imagine how life could go on in the ordinary way, yet we all had things to do the next day.

On Wednesday Roy had to go off to London, just as though nothing had happened, to make another video, this time for Scripture Union. I went across the road to babysit for a neighbour, as arranged. In fact it was the best possible therapy for me: the little girl was quite content as long as I cuddled her, and I felt quite peaceful as I sat for two hours almost without moving, with her relaxed and trusting body warm in my lap. It seemed to me to be a reminder of how safe we can be in the Father's love for us.

At lunchtime I went to see Jim Graham, our pastor. He was very quiet when I told him about Roy; he hugged me and I cried on his shoulder. I think probably he was as shocked as we had been. He said what a godly man Roy is, and how he personally held him in great esteem, and then he suggested that we go into the church and pray. We knelt in front of the communion table, and I was amazed to see him put his arm on the table, lean his head on it, and sob. It was astonishing to me that he could feel so much for Roy— I felt I should comfort him, but I realised that his tears were not so much sadness as a kind of agonising for the situation before the Lord. We prayed together for a while, and then I looked up.

'Jim,' I said, hesitantly, 'I really feel that God is saying something to me. He's saying, "Stand back and see what I am doing. I will bring great glory to my name through this." Am I imagining things? Do you think it's wishful thinking?'

'No,' said Jim. 'I've got very much the same feeling. We're going to have to trust him to bring us all through, and see what his purpose is.'

I was glad he shared my feeling. Deep down I knew it was right: it was a confirmation of what I had sensed the night before, when Roy and Dave were working together and I stood in the kitchen stunned by what had happened but finding God's peace somewhere in the heart of things.

I was grateful for Jim's care. He promised to come and see us later, after he had been to an Elders' meeting. Meanwhile there were other things I had to do: Roy had spent time that morning on the phone, cancelling his trip and other engagements, so I knew that before long the press would get to know what was happening. It was important that I contact the rest of the family before they read about it in the newspapers. We had already planned to ring Daniel in Norway that night; Roy would see Julia in London on Thursday, because we didn't want to tell her by phone if we could avoid it. She was studying for an important exam, but we knew we couldn't put off telling her.

Roy got home early in the afternoon, and at about four o'clock our GP, Tony Welch, arrived.

'Don't go, Fiona,' he said. 'I think you both need to be

here together.' He sat down, clearly finding it hard to say what he needed to say.

'Look,' said Roy, 'we just want the truth. Don't worry about upsetting us—I don't think we can get any more upset now. What will help us most is knowing the facts and what the treatment will be.'

'Roy, I'd love you to prove me wrong by being here in a year's time. But the truth is, even with treatment that isn't very likely. Still, the treatment does offer you the best chance you have, though it isn't pleasant. You may not feel ill now, but once the treatment is under way you're going to feel terrible. The only comfort I can offer you is this: the treatment is designed to kill off the cancer cells. So however bad *you're* feeling, the cancer will be feeling worse!

'The plan is to start on Friday with the first of twelve sessions of chemotherapy—they'll be one a week, and will mean an overnight stay in hospital. Then you'll have two weeks' break, then there'll be five weeks of radiotherapy, five days a week. Those are only short sessions. After that—well, we'll have to see.'

'How does the chemotherapy work?' asked Roy. 'What drugs are they?'

'Oh, that's all worked out by computer,' said Tony. 'We've got a world-wide database for cancer now. We can work out which drugs have been most successful with patients who match your profile exactly—age, medical history, type of cancer and so on. Then a "cocktail" of drugs is calculated to give you the best possible chance of success.'

We could tell that Tony was doing his best to sound positive, but somehow he didn't look very confident. He had known us a long time, and seen our children through all their childhood illnesses, and I could see that he was finding this very hard. Roy was determined to know everything, and went on questioning him closely about the treatment, the side-effects, and the prognosis.

'OK, so that's the treatment,' Roy said at last. 'What if it doesn't work? If I'm going to die of lung cancer—what will it be like? Will it be sudden, or slow? What will the stages be?'

Tony took a deep breath—I don't think he was asked questions like that very often.

'Well, you'd just get progressively weaker. We can keep pain under control with morphine, and your breathing would get more and more difficult and laboured. Then you would probably get very sleepy and slip away.' He swallowed hard. 'Roy—I'm sorry.'

'Oh, well, I just like to know the absolute truth. If we know the worst, we can be prepared, can't we?'

Roy saw Tony to the door with a smile and a joke and then came back into the room.

'It all sounds so awful,' I said, 'I think if I were you I'd just give up and die now, and save yourself all the bother!'

Roy chuckled. 'Well, I suppose we did ask. I'd rather know, wouldn't you?' I nodded, but suddenly I couldn't speak. Tony's explanations had suddenly made it all real— not a nightmare any more. We were part of a system, of hospitals and treatments and the latest research. I was aware of all the other cancer patients and their families who made up the information which would be processed and organised to determine the best treatment for Roy. It was really happening to us—this dreadful disease which had happened to so many other people—and who knew what the outcome would be?

Although we had both agreed that we preferred to know the facts, we went on feeling vaguely depressed all evening. We rang Daniel in Norway and broke the news to him; Roy was too upset to say much and I had to take over the phone and explain everything. Then at about 9.30 the doorbell rang: it was Jim, our minister, and Peter Falconer, one of the church elders. We showed them into the living room.

Jim came straight to the point. 'I was very upset today,

when Fiona told me about your illness, Roy. But this evening I've come in my professional capacity, as your pastor, to pray with you.'

We all sat down, and Jim went on, 'Look what it says in the Bible: "Is any one of you sick? He should call the elders of the church to pray over him and anoint him with oil in the name of the Lord. And the prayer offered in faith will make the sick person well; the Lord will raise him up. If he has sinned, he will be forgiven. Therefore confess your sins to each other and pray for each other so that you may be healed. The prayer of a righteous man is powerful and effective." ' (James 5:14–16)

We prayed together, and then Jim put oil on Roy's forehead and we all laid hands on him. We didn't feel anything spectacular happening, but it was very loving and simple. Jim and Peter did not stay long, as it was getting late and they had been out all evening. The extraordinary thing was that when we were in bed that night, we both realised that we were talking without emotion, and the depression and turmoil we had felt all afternoon had left us. It was as if we had accepted the promise of healing, and all was well and everything had returned to normal. We both felt very peaceful and were able to sleep soundly.

On Thursday morning Roy went up to London early, to catch Julia before she went out. Because she was in the middle of a very demanding course of study we were concerned about telling her, and thought that Roy had better see her. She had bought croissants for their breakfast which they were both too upset to eat—she cried too, but she was very mature about everything and took it very well. I kept to my usual routine of running a Mums and Babies group at the church, called 'Pop-In', and I was fine until the end, when I started explaining to some of the helpers what was happening. I broke down again, and they prayed with me very lovingly. I also had to deal with my speaking engagements. I kept those which were nearby, but cancelled any which involved travelling, as I didn't have any idea how much Roy would need me around in the weeks to come.

On Friday evening I drove Roy to the Thames Valley Nuffield hospital at Wexham for his first treatment. He was installed in bed in a room with a television—it was unlikely that he would get much sleep, as during the treatment there would be regular checks on his temperature and general condition. He was apprehensive but keen to get started, and I left as they were setting up the drip which would deliver the cocktail of chemicals into his bloodstream for the next twenty-four hours.

Downstairs in the hospital lobby, someone called to me just as I was leaving. I turned and saw Roy's specialist hurrying towards me.

'Fiona,' he said, 'I just want you to know that we're giving this our best shot. We do have the very latest technology at our fingertips here, but it's going to be very difficult.' I smiled and thanked him. I knew that he was trying to prepare me for the worst, but I did feel that I had special support and hope in the Lord. Roy and I had prayed together before leaving home, for peace and tranquillity and that the treatment should be effective, and I felt secure as I left him in the hospital.

At home I went to bed, and Roy rang me three times during the night. 'It's still working!' he said cheerfully. He prayed a great deal during the long hours of that night and the next day. He told me later that he had meditated on the cleansing blood of Jesus, which heals us from our sins, and thought of the chemicals in the drip as they passed through his veins, cleansing him from the cancer in the same way. He felt strongly that the skill of the medical profession was a gift of God, to be used to his glory.

I collected him on Saturday evening and took him home. He felt rather woozy from all the drugs, and he looked puffy from the large amounts of liquid which had been passed through his system. He went straight to bed and stayed there the next day, but he was well enough on Monday to get up.

We began to settle into a pattern: on the first week Roy had twenty-four-hour treatment, on the second it was only twelve hours, the third week it was twenty-four hours again. Before each treatment he had to have an X-ray and a blood test, because the drugs which were killing off the cancer cells were also killing off his healthy cells. On one occasion his blood count had not recovered sufficiently, so he had to have a rest from the treatment, and on another he needed a blood transfusion as he was getting so weak.

It was during the third week that Anglia TV put out a press release saying that Roy had been replaced in their forthcoming series about the United States, and of course, all the reporters wanted to know why. Had he been given the sack? Was he getting too old and past it? That Thursday the phone started ringing at 9 pm and went on all evening. Over and over again we explained what was happening, until we felt like answering machines ourselves! At last, at 2 am, peace descended and the phone stopped ringing.

'Thank goodness that's over,' I said. 'Now they've all got their stories and we can have some peace.' We'd had some experience of this sort of thing before—just occasionally when Roy was in the news, there would be a flurry of press activity until all the reporters had filed their stories for the next day's newspapers, and then it would all be over.

I went out the next morning to run another 'Pop-In' session, and got home about noon. To my amazement the house was under siege: the road and the drive were both full of parked cars; when I got into the house the living room was full of reporters, and when I finally reached the kitchen, the sink was full of coffee cups! Roy and Benjamin had spent the whole morning coping with reporters, giving them coffee and answering questions; most of them had been very pleasant, though some were both thoughtless and demanding. At one stage Roy had said that he could really only talk to five of them at a time; one woman had pushed past poor Benjamin at the door, saying, 'I know where to go, I've been here before,' and swept into the living room.

This continued for days, until I began seriously to worry whether it was going to be too tiring for Roy. In fact, after a week or so, I myself began to feel tired and feverish, and promptly went down with the worst case of flu I've ever had. We had been warned that the chemotherapy would reduce Roy's resistance to infection, and that he should stay away from public places as much as possible, and here was I positively breathing germs everywhere! I moved out of the bedroom and slept in the spare room, but it was difficult to keep him clear of infection entirely. I was as hygienic as possible when preparing his food and so on, and only came to his room to bring him meals, but I had to be in the same room as him sometimes!

The other problem was that his illness was so serious (although he did not feel too bad at this stage) that it seemed pathetic for me to complain about a mere virus, even though it was making me feel terrible! In the middle of all this, we had to start filming with the BBC. The science department were making a series called *Fighting Back* about how people coped with different illnesses and their treatment. When they heard that Roy had cancer, they contacted him at once to ask him to make the film on the subject: they had been searching for a well-known figure to use. Roy agreed, but he insisted that whatever the outcome in his particular case, they would pursue it to the end, 'including my funeral if necessary', he said. Among other things, they wanted to film me driving Roy to the hospital for his treatment: Roy was feeling poorly, I was feeling dreadful, the car contained a film crew and all their equipment, and it was bucketing down with rain. I don't think I smiled even once on that piece of film—I just didn't feel able to. There were arms, cameras and sound equipment hanging out of every window; I was trying not to sneeze anywhere in Roy's direction; and generally the whole experience was a nightmare. Then, when we saw the final, edited version of the film, the car could have been anyone's—there was not a single shot of us driving!

I was very hesitant about agreeing to take part in a film about cancer sufferers, but Roy's response was immediate. 'If it's going to help other people to see what happens, we must be willing to go public on it. After all, it says in the Bible, "You are not your own for you have been bought with a great price".' (1 Corinthians 6:19–20) So over the weeks the film crew followed his progress, showing the treatment, talking to doctors, specialists, nurses, and me, to show different aspects of the illness and what the treatment involves. It was only a half-hour programme but they must have filmed enough to make an entire series!

The result of all this was even more attention from the press. We didn't always feel much like giving interviews when Roy felt tired or ill or distressed, but we tried to be as helpful and co-operative as possible. There is no such thing as a private life for a Christian—we should be ready at all times for anything God wants us to do, and to be what he wants us to be. We found that if we were honest and open with the reporters, they were honest in their reporting, and I always prayed before any interview that God would get the glory. I don't know whether that always happened, but I do know that every reporter was told about the reality of our faith in Jesus. We are not to know where that will lead to, whether in the press report or in the writer's personal search for truth and reality.

I have wondered many times about the enormous focus of attention on Roy at that time, and also about the tremendous focusing of prayer by Christians everywhere. Why should we be so privileged? I now believe that it was all part of God's plan for bringing glory to his name. During the Bible holiday weeks called Spring Harvest that Easter 15,000 people wrote on a huge card for Roy—it was filled with the most beautiful and loving messages. It was signed on both sides, stood five feet high and was folded concertina-fashion, stretching across a lawn the size of a tennis court; we thought of wallpapering the house with it. It will be difficult to keep because of its size, but it will be even more difficult to put away because of the love it represents.

Thousands of people wrote to us—one letter was addressed to 'Roy Castle, Entertainer, Huddersfield, Buckinghamshire'! The postman took to delivering in a van because his bicycle could not cope with the bags of mail.

It was an exhausting and time-consuming job trying to answer all these letters personally, but it gave us a daily goal, trying to keep up with it all. Without the letters we would have had much more time to sit around looking at each other and wondering. Instead, there were times when I actually fell asleep half-way through addressing an envelope, and the pen scratched right across the paper! Some days we wrote a hundred letters between us. We put a card table in the living room, and every day that he felt well enough to get up, Roy would sit there to wade through the correspondence. Some people wrote long letters recounting their own experiences, glad to share and aiming to help and offer hope. One woman wrote this, which I found very helpful, and kept: 'Jesus did not come into the world to stop suffering, nor to explain it, nor to take it away, but to fill it with his presence.'

Later on, when Roy's condition began to improve, he was able to help others by writing to them to spur them on to fight with courage and determination to beat 'the bully' as he called it.

Jim and Peter often called late in the evening to pray with us, and they always found us in the same position, with a sea of letters all over the floor and spread on every available surface! The sitting room was constantly chaotic.

Some of the most touching cards were those hand-made by children in an oncology (cancer) ward in a hospital. Childish drawings of Roy doing *Record Breakers* or of their own hospital beds, with scrawled writing saying things like 'Go for it, Roy' 'Don't die—fight for us'. They were so moving, we wept many times over them. These children had their whole lives in prospect. How did they, and their parents, feel? When I looked at those cards I felt thankful for the full lives we had already led.

Roy has turned his hand to most activities in his time, through his role in *Record Breakers*: he has tried parascending, parachuting, wing walking, death slides—he was never afraid to have a try at anything. I think it was partly this great physical courage of his that helped him to be so determined throughout the worst stages of the treatment; but it was also the sense of shared purpose which came from this contact with cancer sufferers all over the world. We were both aware of what a 'taboo' subject cancer is; many people are so afraid of it that they refuse even to say its name. Roy was much taken with one woman's comment, that 'Cancer is a word, not a sentence.' He has used that many times since in talking to people, because he was determined that he would be quite open about what was happening in his efforts to cut cancer down from the monster it appears to be. He also said that he would treat cancer like a heckler in an audience—he would never let it have the last word. (Roy is particularly good with hecklers, as he has a ready supply of comic 'put-downs', a legacy of his years of working in clubs!)

With hindsight we have discovered many good things about the publicity which accompanied Roy throughout his illness. Some of it was sheer hard work for us to deal with, and I was often concerned that Roy was being over-exposed, and that people would be sick of seeing his photos, interviews and TV appearances. But gradually we became aware of how much encouragement his ordeal has given to fellow-sufferers. His ability to joke about the baldness brought on by the chemotherapy and his refusal to hide it has helped many people; similarly his openness about the prognosis he was given, and his courage in facing the pain, discomfort and disruption to everyday life, have helped others to confront their own fears.

Often in the early days I would suggest that Roy should turn down interviews or appearances, partly so that he could conserve his strength. Roy would reply with a shrug of the shoulders:

'It's all in the Lord's hands. He's engineering all this and there must be a reason for it.'

Chapter 6

Gradually the treatment began to take effect, and Roy began to suffer the side effects. First of all, just as we had been warned, his hair began to fall out—not in small amounts, but in handfuls. One night he came out of the bathroom in his dressing gown and called to Antonia.

'Hey, Anto, come up here with your camera, will you? I want a record of this little lot!'

Antonia came upstairs, and there all along the sides of the bath were little clumps of Roy's hair, carefully arranged for a snapshot.

'Gives a whole new meaning to "Wash and Go", doesn't it?' he grinned.

Other side effects were more distressing. First his nails grew thin and brittle, and stopped growing; then his skin became increasingly thin. The chemicals which were stopping the cancer cells from growing and dividing were having the same effect on his healthy cells. The skin at the ends of his fingers began to split, and it was painful for him to pick things up.

'It's a shame my hands are so painful,' he said with a wry smile. 'I'd make a fantastic burglar at the moment: I've got no finger prints!' It was true: the skin had worn away and not been replaced, and the whorled pattern had just disappeared. He had to wear special fine rubber gloves to protect his nerve-endings.

Perhaps the worst, though, were the mouth ulcers. They are often a symptom of being 'run down', and of course Roy was being artificially reduced to a very low level. He developed them all over his tongue, mouth and throat, until he was unable to eat at all. One of his favourite breakfast foods had always been muesli, and I'd been making it with fresh fruit in an effort to increase his intake of health-giving vitamins. Now he was in agony when he tried to eat it, and gradually he had to give up any food which required chewing. Eventually I had to blend all his food like a baby's, and after several weeks he could manage nothing but juices. Fortunately I had bought a juicing machine some years before. Out it came from the attic to do stalwart duty producing gallons of freshly juiced apple and carrot—the blend which seemed to cause least pain.

One of the problems with the chemotherapy was that the effects were patchy—Roy could feel terribly ill one day, and relatively well the next. It was hard to predict how he would feel at any time, so we could never really plan anything properly.

On one occasion he had agreed to appear at an 'Aero-bathon'—a massive aerobics class at the Earls Court Exhibition Centre. The day before, Roy was so ill that he could hardly lift his head off the pillow.

'Roy, you just won't be able to get there tomorrow,' I said to him. 'Let me ring and cancel it—the organisers will be sure to understand. No one can possibly blame you for not being there.'

To my amazement Roy, usually the mildest of men, sat up in a fury.

'Why can't you leave me alone?' he shouted. 'It's my life and my business. Just don't interfere with me. Why don't you get out of the house and never come back?'

I rushed out of the room in tears, and sat downstairs

trying to make sense of what was happening. Was it the drugs making him like this, or just the tension of feeling so ill?

After a few minutes the phone began to ring. When I picked it up, it was Roy on the other end, calling from the bedroom!

'I'm sorry I shouted at you. I don't know what got into me—it was just as if I was standing outside myself watching, but I couldn't stop...Please forgive me!'

After that, I was careful to watch what I said and did, and tried to be aware of what kind of mood he was in. I could tell that Roy was being cautious, too, watching himself for another outburst. Most of the time he was appreciative of all my efforts, but occasionally he would snap at me. I began to see when I was irritating him, by fussing around trying to make him comfortable, or by trying to protect him from doing too much. It was difficult for both of us; it was so out of character for him to be irritable that I would find it hard not to cry. It was unlike me to be so emotional, too, but I couldn't help it. I tried to hide my feelings and went on being very positive for his sake. I became sure that it was the drugs which made him so unreasonable once he had an idea fixed in his mind.

Some things were particularly difficult for me to deal with. I love my husband dearly, and it was agonising to be beside him and watch him suffer. There is a particular kind of pain in being the carer in this situation, and it was only my faith in God which helped me to see my way through these dark days.

On the Sunday before Easter Roy was too ill to go to church, so I went alone. I was praying as I walked along.

'Why, Lord? Isn't it enough that Roy has cancer and has to go through this awful treatment? Why does he have to suffer all these side effects and feel so ill? Couldn't you at least heal those?'

As I prayed it was as if God showed me Jesus in the Garden of Gethsemane. He showed me that Jesus had asked to be spared the pain and horror, the anguish and the indignity—but yet he continued to say that it was the Father's will, not his own human will that he wanted to fulfil. God said, 'See my Son. He did not sidestep the pain: he walked towards it and went through it.'

That was enough to stop me from complaining. Roy himself has said since, 'Whatever I am going through is nothing compared with what Jesus went through. I need to experience everything other cancer patients suffer, to be able to identify with them.'

Roy has had his own path of pain to walk through all this, but to some extent all the family have shared the shock and the fear. We did not have to suffer the trauma of cancer and its treatment, but we had to watch Roy become weaker and weaker, and go through all the distress of seeing him suffer the side effects after every treatment.

One evening Roy was so low and in so much pain that it was all I could do to control my tears. I drove him to the hospital and came home feeling sad and helpless, and longing for someone to talk to. Up in the bedroom I prayed, asking God to cause someone—the right person—to phone and comfort me. I waited and waited, but the phone did not ring, and I realised that God wanted me to cope on my own—that is, on my own with him. I didn't know how to pray so I prayed in tongues, using whatever words the Holy Spirit gave me, 'for we don't even know what we should pray for, but the Holy Spirit prays for us with such feeling that it cannot be expressed in words. And the Father who knows all hearts knows, of course, what the Spirit is saying as he pleads for us in harmony with God's will' (Romans 8:26–27). As I wept it all out to him, he showed me that I didn't need to talk to anyone but him. He has all the answers, and he is the one who cares supremely for his children. Gradually God's peace settled in my heart again, and I found I had new courage and strength to carry on. Even then I knew that this would happen to me many times, as we went through all the ups and downs of Roy's illness, and I resolved to remember the lesson: I only have to take my sorrow to Jesus, because that is where my help lies.

The very next time I was feeling miserable and tired, I asked the Lord to make my prayer more real. The truth was that I was almost too weary to pray, and I felt dull and lifeless. Then I saw in my mind's eye a picture of the back view of Jesus walking slowly along a path with his arm around my shoulder. His head was bent towards me as if he was listening closely to what I had to say, and I felt a great surge of joy. I have tried to hold on to that picture whenever I talk to Jesus about the family's needs and my own, because it reminds me that he will always listen, and take the cares of my heart into his own, and into the heart of the Father.

There was one piece of music I found really helpful during this time. I became very fond of a tape by a Christian singer called Larnelle Harris, and in particular his song, *You're My Child*.

As flowers long for sunshine
And as deserts thirst for rain,
That's how much a father longs
To shield his child from pain.
That's not how life happens,
Still I hope that you will see
That I am never far away
For you're a part of me.
You're my child.

You're my child,
And together we can make a dream,
Though tomorrow may seem far away.
You're my child.

Though at times it seems so hard for you to know
Just how far love will go.
Oh it's strong enough to reach across the years,
Through the joys, through the tears,
You're my child.

With words I've said I love you
To express the way I feel,
But the scars can run so deep
That words alone can't heal.
The joy in our tomorrows
Rests in finding Christ today,
And then our happiness is found
Each time we hear him say—

You're my child,
And together we can make a dream.
Though tomorrow may seem far away
You're my child.
Though at times it seems so hard for you to know
Just how far love will go.
Oh it's strong enough to reach across the years,
Through the joys, through the tears,
You're my child.

I listened to that tape as I did the housework and sometimes as I was driving the car, and it always helped to
reassure me. We are God's children and he does care for us;
as Christians we do know 'just how far love will go'—it
went as far as death on the cross when Jesus died for our
sins and rose again. I know that 'through the joys, through
the tears' I am God's child.

Something I noticed particularly during the difficult
times of Roy's illness was that I did not seem to suffer from
the kind of depression I had before I became a Christian. In
those days I really had very little to be depressed about,
other than the ordinary tiredness which comes with four
small children, yet I continually felt low and over-anxious,

full of self-pity and anger. Now I really had something to worry about, yet I would not describe it as 'depression'. It was more a mixture of sadness and helplessness, and although I occasionally felt tearful and upset, I always knew that I could take my troubles to the Lord. The security and confidence that gave me enabled me to be cheerful and buoyant most of the time, and we laughed a great deal through all the inconveniences and difficulties of the illness.

One well-meaning correspondent wrote to me, 'You don't realise what a privilege it is for you to serve Roy at this time.' This immediately became a family joke, and when I brought Roy his breakfast, he would say, 'Thank you, darling. I hope you realise what a privilege it is for you to bring me my breakfast!'

It was good to know, too, that friends were praying for us. Once we knew what was wrong with Roy, one of the first people we told was Harry Secombe. He had been a close friend for a very long time, and Roy wanted to ring him personally. He told Harry 'It's quite likely that I'm going to die', and they both got very upset. Harry was marvellous during Roy's treatment, turning up with arm-fuls of books and flowers to cheer him up (and judging from the laughter coming from the bedroom, succeeding very well!). At one stage when we were both feeling very tired and worn out by the routine of treatment, Harry and his wife invited us to visit them for a day, so that we could get away from the house, and they even sent a car to collect us so that we wouldn't have to drive.

Another Christian friend who was very supportive was Cliff Richard—he rang regularly to check how Roy was feeling, and we knew that he, too, was praying for us.

Many of Roy's show business friends are comics; when they visited or telephoned it was hard to believe that they were commiserating with a very sick man—the jokes would fly thick and fast and everyone would be laughing together.

Norman Wisdom had known us for years, and so had Roy Hudd; I'm sure that their laughter did Roy more good than almost anything else. It certainly took our minds off our troubles to have these two clowning around, and we appreciated the concern that led them to take time to phone us.

Dora Bryan was another long-time friend who kept in close touch during these weeks. When Roy was feeling too ill to get up he found the long days in bed very dull, and that was when the phone calls from Dora and others were a real bonus.

'It's taught me a lesson,' Roy said to me one day. 'You know, before all this happened, if ever I heard that someone was ill, I'd think, "What a shame," but I probably wouldn't do anything about it. I wouldn't even have expected that someone who was ill would want to hear from me. But now I realise just how important it is. I'm so grateful when friends call in or write or phone—it really brightens up the day!'

Show business people are so often seen on stage alone, or in a particular role, that the public seldom realise how many firm friendships exist behind the scenes. Many of these friendships go back years to harder times when they were not such famous names, playing summer seasons together or sharing scruffy digs. Nowadays, of course, they are quite unimpressed by one another's fame or success, and carry on joking together just as they always did.

Another morale-booster for Roy was the warm reception he was given by the public whenever he was well enough to appear at events. He was scheduled to appear on a TV series called *Bruce and Friends* with Bruce Forsyth, who is another old friend. When Roy was ill, Bruce kindly invited Benjamin to appear instead, which was a great break for Benj, as he was able to play his saxophone while Bruce played the piano. On the day, Roy was feeling fairly well, so he turned up at the last minute and joined them on stage after Benj had played. He got such a huge round of applause from the audience that he could hardly contain the tears—people were so pleased to see him.

Receiving that kind of support is a special privilege when you are in show business; the price you have to pay for it is the unremitting pressure of the publicity. We had always known that the attention of the press was part of our lifestyle, and we didn't complain about it. But it is hard for anyone outside the situation to understand how exhausting it can be, at a time of illness and great stress, to have to have a 'public' face for the press. During those weeks I never put the coffee cups away; as soon as I washed up I put them straight back on the tray, which I kept laid with a coffee pot, because I knew there would always be another reporter at the door asking for an interview. There were photographers outside our door even on Christmas Day— just to see what the Castle family were doing at Christmas.

On the whole, though, we were immensely grateful for all the interest and concern and love that seemed to surround us. Both strangers and friends wrote and telephoned and showed that they cared in many ways, sending everything from flowers to advice.

Not all the advice we were offered was helpful, though well-intentioned. For instance, we knew from the specialists that Roy could expect to start losing his hair after the third week of chemotherapy: the hair becomes weak and breaks off just above the follicle. A few Christian friends were convinced that this did not have to be the case; they were sure that if we prayed, God would preserve Roy's hair, and they said that they knew of other cases where this had happened. When his hair fell out, right on cue, I felt that people would think that I didn't have enough faith. Then we heard that only certain types of medication have this effect on the hair. The instances where the 'faithful' didn't suffer hair loss could equally have been the result of different drugs. Even as I felt released from my feelings of guilt, I began to see how silly the whole thing was. Why should we set up hoops for our prayer lives to jump through? God isn't trying to play games with us, or set us targets of this much or that much faith.

Often as Christians we become so introspective that anything can become an occasion for feelings of guilt. Am I feeling low, or depressed? Then at once I add to my burden by feeling guilty as well, because 'Christians should be full of joy', so I must be lacking in faith. In fact, it may not be faith that is lacking so much as a good night's sleep or a square meal! After all, we are physical creatures as well as spiritual ones. I have learned not to be swayed too much by my feelings, and not to mistake temporary states of health or mood for spiritual crises.

I have found one solution for this. If I concentrate on thinking about others, and refuse to analyse my feelings too deeply, I remove the focus from myself, and also remove the tendency to self-pity or guilt. I learned this years ago in the days when I was looking after the children more or less single-handed. When I was totally exhausted it was tempting to wallow in the luxury of self-pity, and I would often make a conscious decision to go to bed and not to think about things at all until morning. I knew that when my emotions were unbalanced and irrational there was no point in mulling things over endlessly. I have known people who were so analytical about everything that they took all the spontaneity and fun out of life. Self-consciously looking at all their reactions, they worried endlessly about their faith or lack of it, and were racked by guilt, often quite unnecessarily.

On the other hand, I was brought up in a household where common sense and discipline were of the essence, and I inherited plenty of both. It was only much later that I realised that a little applied psychology could also be very helpful, especially when dealing with children. Two books which helped me a great deal were *How to really love your child* and *How to really love your teenager*, by Dr Ross Campbell. From them I learned the importance of giving a child your undivided attention, including eye contact, rather than always doing something else when you are with them. These books helped me to focus on the positive, rather than the negative aspects of family life, and also to be prepared for some of the pitfalls that awaited me as they grew up.

Nowadays I feel that a healthy balance is best: understand something about how your mind works and what your motivation might be, and then use your common sense. As Roy says, 'Moderation in all things!' This has certainly been true in dealing with his cancer: having faith in the midst of trauma, without the guilt of feeling that we should be doing better if we went into things more deeply.

Before every session of chemotherapy Roy had to have an X-ray, to check whether the treatment was still working. The X-ray before the final scheduled session showed that the tumour had shrunk away until it was almost invisible. When I heard the news I didn't get terribly excited, not because I didn't believe it, but because I had believed it all along. I felt rather like saying, 'Well of course, what else did you expect?' I wasn't being presumptuous. In a way I suppose God was keeping me on an even keel, because I had complete trust in him for the outcome of the treatment.

This was one of the many times when I have been grateful for a simple, straightforward faith. There were no complications in it, just continuous supplication to the throne of God—for protection during the medication and treatment, for skill and wisdom for the medical profession, and for God's healing to flow through these channels.

This is another area where some Christians seem to have differing views. I have met people who say that they refuse to call a doctor if a member of the family is ill, but rely only on prayer. They suggest that to rely on human medication is a sign of a lack of faith.

I find this a troubling area, for I believe in God's ability to heal people directly, and I have witnessed people being healed. I consulted a wise pastor friend about this, and asked him if it showed a lack of faith to rely on medicine rather than on miraculous 'divine healing'. He replied, 'Unless you get a clear word from the Lord specifically saying that God will heal in this case through a miracle, you should not depend upon it.'

I found this a great comfort, and I am sure that we did the right thing in choosing to let God heal Roy through the medical profession. In fact, Roy refuses to say 'God has healed me'. He says that the cancer might recur next week and he might die—and what would that do to the faith of anyone who trusted his words? It may well be that God has healed him for a while only, and will call him to himself in his own time. Roy says that he knows that God is in control, but he also knows that the doctors' skill is a gift of God.

'We're in God's hands,' he says. 'We're not doubting; we're trusting totally that God has a plan and a purpose in this. Anyone who wants to dispute it can deal with him!' We feel that we are giving God the glory when we show we are trusting him, whether or not Roy is healed.

Roy's security and simple faith in God have been an enormous help to me, especially throughout this crisis in our lives. The one thing which has become clearer and clearer to us is the importance of trusting God and knowing his word through reading the Bible, and this applies equally for the major events in life and for the everyday things. One day I was wondering where to put a visitor since the spare room was already occupied. Roy looked up and grinned. 'My Bible reading this morning says, "Get into the habit of inviting friends round for a meal, and if they need somewhere to sleep, for the night as well." Maybe we ought to buy another spare bed!'

We have always been very different in our approach to

things and for a long time we seldom prayed together, because I was very wary of being 'pushy' about my new-found faith. Roy has appreciated this because my style is so different from his; so often I study and pray and agonise my way into some new idea, only to find that Roy has been there for years, patiently waiting for me to catch up!

Our experience of the Holy Spirit was rather like this. Before I became a Christian I didn't understand about him at all; I usually referred to him as 'it', and couldn't quite see the role of the third Person of the Trinity. After I had become a Christian I had several dreams about the Holy Spirit, from which I would wake up aware that someone had been with me, but still not understanding much. I didn't like to speak to Roy about it, as I was still being very cautious in case he thought I was becoming a religious maniac! I questioned Tamara, the friend who had led me to Jesus, and she promised that we would get together and pray about it.

'Actually,' she added, 'I don't think you really need to. I believe that you are already filled with the Spirit—I've seen you several times showing the sort of wisdom you couldn't naturally show. That wisdom is one of the gifts of the Spirit. But don't worry, I'll explain it all when I see you.'

Meanwhile, with a spark of inspiration, I had decided that it was all very well ringing up Tamara with my questions, but what about ringing up God? So I found a book on the subject (*The Holy Spirit and You* by Dennis Bennett), and got down on my knees for a conversation with God.

'Lord, if you have filled me with your Spirit, please show me. I'm a very new Christian, and I need a sign of confirmation that this is true. Please give me the gift of "tongues".'

As I prayed and praised God, I found a strange word came into my mouth. As soon as I had spoken it, I thought, 'How silly—it must just be me making it up.' Somehow the idea struck me as funny and I began to giggle. As I laughed, more words came, and there I was, speaking in tongues and laughing at the same time. If anyone had seen or heard me I'm sure they would have thought that I was crazy, talking in the strange language the Lord had given me, in between giggles.

The next day I phoned Tamara. 'You were right,' I said, 'I've already got it!'

However, when I finally spoke to Roy about it, he was his usual calm self. He, too, has been filled with the Holy Spirit but he has never spoken in tongues. 'Well, I don't need a sign that he's in me, do I?' he says. One of Roy's spiritual gifts is an astounding ability to go straight to the heart of a problem, and a wisdom in dealing with people which is wonderful to see, together with a great assurance of faith.

There was one occasion when we were together at a speaking engagement in Bristol, and invited questions from the floor. One woman called out to him, 'When did you become a Christian and what was your experience?'

'Well, I can't tell you the exact date when I became a Christian,' began Roy.

'Then I would question whether you really are a Christian,' retorted the woman.

We were both deeply hurt by that response. So many people seem to think that theirs is the only acceptable form of experience, as though the Lord were not capable of dealing with each of us in an infinite variety of ways. And with so much for us to do in this world to preach the gospel, it makes us very sad that some Christians are more concerned with tearing down than with building up. As Roy says, 'I question no one's faith, but I do ask, what does their faith make them do?'

The Bible tells us to love and support one another: 'But you, dear friends, build yourselves up in your most holy faith and pray in the Holy Spirit. Keep yourselves in God's love as you wait for the mercy of our Lord Jesus Christ to bring you to eternal life.' We give thanks for the many friends who have supported us with love and prayer throughout this time, and for the pastors and elders of our church who have dealt with us with wisdom and kindness.

Chapter 7

After the course of chemotherapy had finished, Roy expected to start feeling better. Unfortunately, some of the early side effects returned, particularly the mouth ulcers which had made him feel so wretched, though they were not so bad this time. It meant that the three-week break before the radiotherapy began was not quite the holiday he had hoped for.

The chemotherapy kills off cancer cells via the bloodstream; the radiotherapy was necessary to finish off the tumour. However, the treatment was not nearly so devastating as the chemotherapy had been. Roy's skin would be marked with ink so that the target site was clearly visible; then he was told not to move, the machine was lined up with great precision and the ray directed at the tumour. Apart from feeling rather tired, and developing a mark rather like sunburn on his skin, Roy felt no apparent side effects of the radiotherapy at the time, and gradually he felt better and better. He was able to drive himself to and from the hospital, and since the whole business took only about fifteen minutes, it became a routine afternoon outing which he dealt with alone. He enjoyed being independent again.

Because it was an outpatient procedure, Roy would meet other patients in the reception area, waiting for their turn in the treatment room. They chatted among themselves and it soon became clear that it was rather like a sort of cancer patients' club meeting—enlivened, no doubt, by Roy's humour. One man was known as the Tapioca King because his illness meant that the only food he could swallow was tinned tapioca. He confessed that he used to visit several different supermarkets and shops a week, so that the shop assistants wouldn't wonder at the number of tins of tapioca he was buying. Another man said that he was rather sorry that his course of radiotherapy finished before Roy's, as he enjoyed their afternoons so much!

Throughout the whole of his treatment Roy's attitude had been very buoyant. He was determined not to give in to self-pity or bitterness. Many years ago I recall him saying to me, 'Why can't people think of what they have, instead of what they haven't?' He repeated this in a different way recently, when discussing someone we know who has a few problems in her marriage. 'I imagine she's a person that many people envy, because she has everything most people would long for: a faithful husband and a lovely home with a pretty garden, healthy and intelligent children, enough money to supply all her needs and enjoy luxury holidays. Why can't she focus on all those and be grateful for the situation she's in, instead of complaining about the things that aren't perfect?'

It seems we so quickly latch on to the negatives in our lives, when in fact they are heavily weighted with positive things. So many people have so much less than we do, yet we take all our blessings for granted and whine when they are taken away. Health is one of those blessings. When someone said to Roy, 'It's so unfair—why does it have to be you?' he replied, 'Why not me? I'm just the same as anyone else.'

Roy never dwelt on his problems and constantly made light of them, and an air of optimism and laughter prevailed in our home through even the darkest days. We were glad there was no remorse. This wasn't a grim determination to 'exhibit Christian joy' even if it killed us—rather the fact that in the face of death every moment was precious, and the present came into sharp focus. We laughed more than we had ever done; trivialities such as bad weather and late trains were mild irritants when it was a joy to be alive and fit enough to stand in the rain. It sometimes takes a crisis to put life and our priorities into perspective.

This was something we had learned the hard way some years before, when Daniel had an accident. We were all in the Isle of Man together—Roy was working there and I had taken the family up to join him for a holiday. God had prepared us for a family crisis earlier that day: we had already witnessed another accident in which some horses had injured a group of people. The children had been very shaken by what they had seen, and kept talking about it and going over it again and again. Eventually I had said to them, 'Look, just put it out of your minds and talk about something else. If you find you keep thinking about what you saw, just ask Jesus to take away those pictures and replace them with something lovely.'

That worked for a few minutes and then they started discussing it all over again. I turned to Roy.

'We must get the children talking about something else,' I said. 'Let's go and find something for them to do.'

'No, I don't think so,' said Roy. 'It's far healthier if they can talk it out of their system. Let them work through it in their own way.'

So we went through it all again, and in the end I said to them, 'You know, the Bible teaches us that we have to be prepared to face death at every moment of our lives. We're happy now—we're all well and we're all together, but we don't know what may happen next week or next year. Let's give thanks to God for this moment when we're all together as a happy family, and be prepared to accept whatever God gives us in the future.' They were prophetic words, for within half an hour Daniel's life was hanging in the balance.

We had gone for a walk on an isolated beach, and Daniel had climbed up the cliff and was sitting watching the rest of us beachcombing. We were all strolling along, heads down and looking at the sand, when Antonia screamed, 'Daniel!' We turned and saw Daniel lying on the rock in the strangest position, in a sort of ball with his legs over his head. He must have slipped and fallen some thirty feet, somehow somersaulting so that his feet were above his head. We knew that you should not move an injured person, but we had to uncurl him or he would have suffocated. There were a few other people on the cliff, and someone ran to call an ambulance at once, but when it arrived the ambulance men realised that they could not drive down to the beach because there had been a landslip.

As we sat with Daniel, Antonia said to me, through her tears, 'Mummy, why aren't you crying?' The truth was that some emotions are too deep for tears, and in fact it was six months before I was able to release the fear and trauma of that accident enough to weep over it.

Meanwhile Daniel was looking greyer and colder, and blood was trickling from his mouth and his ears. I was sure he had a serious head injury. An ambulance man stayed with us, taking Daniel's pulse at intervals and giving him oxygen while the ambulance drove away to the next beach. A lifeboat was dispatched to our cove—the only way it could be approached was by sea—and we were left to wait for help to come.

That very morning I had been reading my Bible and praying, and I had found one thought returning again and again, in a way I was beginning to recognise. I'm not usually very good at writing things down, but this time I felt God was teaching me something important, so I wrote it down in the front of my Bible: 'Christian joy is not dependent on worldly happiness—worldly happiness is

dependent on everything being right and going smoothly.'
It makes good sense; if everything in your life is going right,
it's easy to be happy; but if something bad happens, then
you become depressed and worried. I had to realise,
immediately that accident happened, that my joy was not
dependent on worldly circumstances, on what was happening around me, but it was dependent on my life in Christ.
Nothing could shift the life of Christ inside me and his love
for me, and so my joy would continue through everything.

We could have been a forlorn little group, gathered
around Daniel's unconscious body as we waited on the
beach for the rescue party. But we sang songs praising God
and thanking him for his fatherly care, for the Bible tells us
'In all things give thanks and rejoice always'—not just in
the good times, but always. We didn't feel much in the
mood for rejoicing, but we sang all the choruses we could
think of, in a spirit of obedience. We knew that we had a
Father who cared for us and for Daniel, and that we were
all safe in his hands, whatever happened.

When the lifeboat arrived it brought a kind of sling,
rather than a stretcher, rather like a shopping basket. The
men had to load Daniel's limp body into it and wade out
through the waves to the boat. Roy helped to carry him out
to the boat, and travelled round to the next bay where the
ambulance was waiting to take him on the twenty-minute
journey to hospital. The whole rescue had taken two
hours—two hours in which Daniel's life seemed to be
ebbing away. The ambulance man who rode in the boat
with Roy was constantly monitoring his breathing and
pulse, and kept shaking his head and giving Roy looks
which combined sympathy and hopelessness.

At the hospital they cut Daniel out of his clothes and
X-rayed him. They told us that he had fractured his skull,
his pelvis and his wrist; he had also broken a rib which had
punctured his lung. I remember helping to push the trolley
from the X-ray department to the intensive care ward,

where he was wired up to lots of monitoring machinery which bleeped endlessly. All along the corridor there were 'fire door' notices saying 'No Escape'; I felt as if the Lord was telling me clearly that I could not hide from this—I had to face up to my problems.

As we sat beside his bed all that night, we realised that Daniel's head injuries were so severe that he might well die. Even if he recovered, no one could tell us how much brain damage there might be. There was little we could do other than sit beside him and pray; we did ring Jim Graham at home and tell him what had happened, and he told our church 'prayer chain', in which urgent news is passed by telephone, so that soon the whole fellowship was praying for Daniel. I remember going into the waiting room outside the intensive care unit and finding myself repeating the words from Job, 'The Lord giveth and the Lord taketh away; blessed be the name of the Lord' (Job 1:21).

The following day our assistant pastor at that time, Justin Dennison, and Malcolm Richards, an elder of the church, flew to the Isle of Man to join us; by the time they arrived Daniel had been delirious for almost thirty-six hours, and he had not fully regained consciousness. We stood around his bed and prayed, and Justin and Malcolm anointed him with the oil they had brought with them. During the prayer Daniel continued to toss and mutter in his delirium, but at the end of the prayer he opened his eyes, looked up and said, quite clearly, 'Amen'.

I knew that moment was the beginning of his healing, and when he closed his eyes again I could see that he was sleeping normally, and had not relapsed into unconsciousness. The nursing he received in the following weeks he spent in the hospital was magnificent—it was the unit which dealt with all injuries in the famous TT motorcycle races in the Isle of Man—but I still believe that his healing was a miracle. We knew that God had everything in control, because he was in control of our lives. 'We know that all that happens to us is working for our good if we love God and are fitting into his plans' (Romans 8:28). We knew that we loved God and that he loved us and that he would not let us go. That didn't mean that we were sure that Daniel would be made whole: we didn't know whether God would take Daniel to himself, but we had to let go of him and place him in God's hands, and accept the Father's will, whatever that meant for us.

Even as Daniel's healing began, I realised that we had had our priorities wrong in the past. I had been nagging Daniel about working hard for his O levels, but after the accident I found that I didn't care whether he ever passed an exam again—there's nothing in the Bible that says you have to have eight O levels to be a child of God! We were so delighted when he was able to say his first words to us; when he began hobbling around and then walking properly; when he laughed again. None of us had known for sure that he would ever do any of these things again.

We were so thankful for this miracle that we asked God to use it for his glory. I later read some words by Oswald Chambers that seemed to relate to this: 'If God can bring his purposes to pass through a broken heart, then thank him for that broken heart!' I realised that all our priorities had been changed through Daniel's accident, terrible though it was at the time, and our whole family came into a new appreciation of each other and the daily blessings of life and health. The important thing is not what happens to you, but how you deal with what happens.

In the same way, the important thing about Roy's illness was how we dealt with it. We could have turned our backs on God in bitterness and self-pity, or we could go on trusting him and working with him, trying to do his will.

One of the difficulties, sometimes, is finding God's will for us. Too often we waste time looking around for some great act that we can do for God, to show him how willing we are to do his will, when the real challenges are right in front of us. I can't begin to analyse why we have been so blessed in our circumstances, but I do know that God expects me to do what he wants me to do in the circumstances where he has placed me.

One phrase I grew up with was 'Much is expected of those to whom much is given'—it shaped my thinking long before I had a relationship with Jesus. My mother and father took it very seriously and passed it on to me, along with other ideas like 'You only get out of life what you put in'; 'If you have a lot you must give a lot'; 'Be acceptable to other people'; and 'Always think of others as better than yourself.' I think many of these phrases had a biblical origin. The only one which I am sure was not biblical was one which unfortunately I firmly believed for many years: 'You must try hard to be good if you want to go to heaven.' It was simplistic, but an impossible task, and of course I failed miserably in my own eyes and, I am sure, in God's. I tried hard to earn 'Brownie points' so that God could count them up at the end and say, 'OK, that'll do, you're in.' I suppose this attitude developed a strong moral conscience, but it didn't bring me happiness or confidence in God's love. I didn't gain that until I stopped trying in my own strength and learned to rely on Jesus to give me eternal life.

Nowadays I have laid aside the question of why I was born into such a blessed situation, to be answered in eternity. I consider it more important to go on and make the most of everything I do, asking God to show me his will in everything. 'Blossom where you are planted' is good advice; or, as my Bible study notes once put it, 'You may as well be useful to God where you are, for you certainly are of no use where you are not!' That speaks to me constantly and enables me to take one day at a time in confidence that God will guide me to do his will.

One of my many faults, and one which I suspect I share with many people, is that I am very independent. I love to give of my time and energy to others, but I'm not so good at being on the receiving end. In the early days of Roy's cancer, most of the friends who phoned us said, 'If there's anything we can do to help, just ask.' If they were Christians, we simply asked them to pray; otherwise we said thank you and that we would let them know. I know that if our positions had been reversed, I would have made the same offer, and I would have been pleased and flattered if the person had accepted, and asked me to do any small service which would enable me to express my love and caring. However, in fact I found it hard to think of anything which other people could help with. Perhaps it's just that when we're under stress it takes almost more energy to delegate a job than to do it ourselves. As it was, I just got on with what had to be done, hour by hour and day by day. If our children had been younger then I imagine it would have been a great help if someone had done the school run or taken them out to tea, but as things were I was able to do the driving and shopping. Even when Roy was in bed I was able to cope with the day-to-day chores by fitting them round his schedule. I now think that perhaps the best kind of offer of help would have been a specific one, so that I didn't have to stop and try to think about what needed doing. The person who turns up with a home-made cake, or who commandeers the kitchen and unobtrusively does the ironing or the washing up without making an issue of it, is a real help to the carer.

As time went on, and Roy went through the treatments, we became gradually accustomed to what was happening to us, to the extent that we almost became casual about the whole episode. There were still days when I thought my heart would break and that I would explode with the grief and helplessness of it all, but on the whole the time passed quickly as I coped with daily duties and needs as they arose. It is as if the human heart can only bear so much agony and hurt, and we take refuge in normal life.

All the way through the last months I have often thought, 'Well, I wouldn't be without this experience.' I felt that it was changing me, my attitude to life, to other people, and particularly my ability to identify with others who are in pain or grief. I have long felt that it was impertinent to say, 'I know just how you feel, and what you're going through,' when clearly I didn't know at all.

This was brought home to me at the time of my father's death, when well-meaning friends and neighbours often failed to offer any real comfort because they couldn't really understand how I felt. Another thing I learned at this time was how important it is to confront people who are suffering bereavement or trauma, to give them the choice of talking about it or changing the subject. After my father died, I saw people cross the street rather than face me or mention my father to me. I found this very hurtful until I realised that I had at times done the very same thing. I had acted this way not because I didn't care, but because I didn't understand how much a bereaved person may need and long to talk about the dead person. I felt inadequate, and sure that I wouldn't know the right things to say, and embarrassed in the face of other people's emotions. I realised then that avoiding people only deepens the isolation and sense of loss they may be feeling. I resolved that whenever I knew someone in a similar situation, I would always approach them, even if I could only hug them.

Long after my father's death, I picked up a little card at a Christian meeting which expressed all this exactly:

I'm there if you need me.
I can't pretend that I know what you're going through,
And it would be so easy to be glib.
But I am sure you know I mean it when I say
I'm always thinking of you.
I am here any time you need me
If you need a shoulder to cry on
Or someone to hold you close

Maybe just to run an errand or help in any other way.
Whatever it may be, please don't think no one cares—
And—who knows—one day
I may need you, so please let me show you how much you
      mean
And make it easier for me.
      A Friend.

(Humfrey Temple, Christian Art Ltd 1991)

During Roy's illness I discovered a further truth about how to minister to others in these times of trauma. It is one thing to brace ourselves to face someone who is in pain, and ask them how they are feeling, but a great deal depends on the way we ask the question. Asking someone, 'Well, how are you today, all right?' in a breezy fashion rather demands a positive answer, and blocks the way to a real conversation.

There was one day when I was feeling really low, tired and emotionally drained. I wanted to sit down and sob, and I knew I would if anyone gave me half a chance! A friend called in to see Roy, and came into the kitchen on his way out. He sat down for a while to talk to me, and although he asked me how I was, I found I couldn't tell him. I could only reply, 'Oh, I'm fine,' which was a complete lie. I suppose I felt that I would be letting the side down if I showed any sign of strain. What I really wanted to do was cry on someone's shoulder, but perhaps deep down I felt that he couldn't have coped with that.

It has taught me an important lesson, that sometimes it is necessary to ask a second question, to make it clear that we are willing to hear the bad side of things, without prying or being intrusive; 'Are you feeling down today?'

I am sure that there are important lessons for us all to learn about how to offer sympathy to each other, and how to do it in a sensitive way. In particular, the role of the carer can sometimes be a lonely one, when all attention is focused (quite rightly) on the sufferer and his treatment. This is where church fellowships can come into their own with a varied range of ministries, from physical help where that is needed, to emotional support for someone who needs simply to let some of the emotion out occasionally. Not all Christians, however well-meaning, are good at this kind of sensitivity.

One piece of advice, for which we were always grateful, came from our pastor, Jim Graham. He has always been very good at letting us be ordinary members of the congregation—which of course we are—and completely ignoring the fact that Roy is well known outside church. However, on one occasion at the end of a service he quite uncharacteristically singled us out and addressed us in front of the whole congregation.

'Now that so many people know you are ill, Roy,' he said, 'you will receive lots of comments, advice and information from many sources. Some of it will be helpful, some of it will be unhelpful, and both sorts will come from other Christians. I want to reassure you that whatever the future holds for you, I and this fellowship are standing with you and rooting for you.' This proved to be a real support to us, as with this forewarning we were not so troubled as we might have been when the odder letters and suggestions started arriving. One lady wrote and said that she had had many friends who had suffered from cancer and they had all died! Several people wrote to Roy and told him that his illness was due to some unconfessed sin in his life, and that the evil inherent in show business was the cause.

Several writers claimed to have prophetic words from God—some including explicit instructions about the cabaret appearances Roy should give for the writer!—and sent books on obedience as an added spur to encourage Roy to follow their instructions. We were not swayed by all this advice from so many quarters, as we felt we had a scripture from God in James 5: 'Is anyone sick? He should call for the elders of the church and they should pray over him and pour a little oil upon him, calling on the Lord to heal him.

And their prayer, if offered in faith, will heal him, for the Lord will make him well' (James 5:14,15).

Some of the very distressing letters I threw away without ever letting Roy see them. I would not normally censor his mail, but I felt justified in the face of some of the unqualified venom which these letters displayed. It was clear that there would be no benefit to anyone from reading them or from replying to them, though I prayed for the senders who evidently had many problems of their own.

These letters, however, were in the minority. Most of the communications we received were sent in love and hope, enclosing books, cassettes, videos, leaflets, diet sheets, pictures of saints—almost anything people could think of that might be of help or support to us. It reminded me again of the time of Daniel's accident. Then, too, when his accident was mentioned in the national press we were deluged with letters expressing love, concern and prayer. I had spent two days and two nights constantly at his bedside, and when I returned to the hotel for some sleep, Roy took my place. As soon as I arrived the phone began ringing, and the hotel delivered stacks of mail to our room. We were surrounded by interest and affection. I felt as if God was saying, '*Now* will you believe that I love you?' I realised then that God expresses his love for us in many different ways—not just in his provision for us but through the actions of other people. And just as we benefit from the expression of that love by others, so we have to learn to be God's love for our fellows. As St Theresa wrote:

> Christ has no body now on earth but yours,
> No hands but yours,
> No feet but yours.
> Yours are the eyes through which is to look out Christ's
>   compassion to the world.
> Yours are the feet with which he is to go about doing good.
> Yours are the hands with which he is to bless men now.

Chapter 8

On the whole, cancer patients are encouraged to work whenever they feel well enough to do so; in Roy's case this was not so easy as his work is usually planned many months in advance. There was no way he could book a summer season when he was undergoing treatment, since he never knew how well he would be feeling, or indeed, whether he would still be alive to do it. However, once his condition became known he received many requests from charities to open fetes, make guest appearances or perform at fund-raising concerts. He was delighted to accept many of these, for two reasons: firstly, because he was keen to help any charities, especially those for cancer research or supporting sufferers; and secondly, because it helped him to be busy and feel useful. He could not accept professional contracts because of the real risk that he would simply be too ill to fulfil them; charity events, for which he would not be paid, he could accept on the basis that the organisers understood that he might be too ill to attend when the time came. The only professional work he did take on was the BBC film, which he went on making throughout his treatment.

I have often recalled those words God gave me, 'Stand back and see what I am going to do.' As time has gone on I have been able to see more and more of God's plan unfolding. As well as the changes that God has wrought in us individually, and the incalculable effects of our witness to his fatherly love, we have seen that Roy has developed a role in publicising the dangers of smoking.

For many years Roy had been asking the Lord to use him, and he had always received the answer, 'Just wait.' He wanted something real so that no one could doubt the truth of what he was saying—but I don't think he ever expected the answer to that prayer to come through suffering from cancer! He has been given a platform to speak out against the dangers of smoking—something he has always done, but now he speaks with far greater authority. He has the added influence of the doctors' conclusion that passive smoking can cause lung cancer, backed up by his own experience as a non-smoker with the disease.

On one occasion he went with his oncologist to speak to a House of Commons meeting about passive smoking, and he makes many visits to schools to talk to school children about the dangers. This year, for the second time, he appeared at the Earl's Court Aerobathon in aid of the Royal Marsden Hospital appeal. Last year he promised the organisers that if he survived, he would return 'with hair'! The event broke the record for the largest number of people at an aerobics class in one place, and over £1 million was raised. He has also made a recording for the same charity, of 'Somewhere over the rainbow'. He is fully booked for months ahead for charity events, and we are still receiving hundreds of letters requesting personal appearances or cabaret acts in aid of various cancer charities. In fact, he has now been declared fit for professional work, and his agent is once again working at full stretch packing in the professional bookings.

Although Roy's life is back to normal as far as work is concerned, he still finds time to answer the many personal letters which come to him from or on behalf of cancer sufferers. Often people write to him saying, 'My sister (or aunt, or husband) has cancer and is feeling very low. A phone call from you would really cheer her up.' He usually answers requests like that at once, often chivvying busy hospital staff to put him through to patients in the ward. He knows that in the bad times, a cheering word can be very important, and that it can't wait. He recalls how much he gained from the helpful letters he received when he was ill. There was one man in particular, a musician, with whom Roy is still in touch, who had been through a similar treatment. He often wrote to Roy, saying, 'You'll feel like this for a while...or you'll have these symptoms...but it's only a phase and you'll come through it.' At stages when he felt really awful, it was a real help to know that it wouldn't last for long.

Some people have written to say how much they appreciated hearing from Roy, and that they carry his letter around with them all the time. It is a strange thing, to have the power to affect people in this way; it is conferred partly by his fame and television appearances, and partly by his ability to make jokes and cheer people up with his irrepressible humour. But most of all, I think, he is able to help people because he has stood where they are standing; they know that he truly understands what they are going through, and he is able to speak to their hearts when he tells of his trust in God.

Roy has already outlived the first prognosis he was given. Not only that, but he appears to be as well and energetic as ever, so that it is hard to believe that he must be constantly monitored for some time. The radiotherapy left him with a chronic cough (he didn't have a cough when the cancer was diagnosed) as the dead cells inside his lungs are sloughed away.

After his final session of radiotherapy there was a three-week break, and then he had another scan and bronchoscopy to test his lung tissue. I was so sure of Roy's healing by then that it was a real shock when the doctors told us that they had found some cancer cells still in his lung. There was no evidence that they were growing, but it meant that Roy was by no means declared clear of cancer. I had been all ready to shout to the world that Roy had been healed, and the news was a shocking blow. For several days I felt very depressed and disappointed. During those few days I seemed to be constantly reminded about death—I heard programmes on the radio about widows, and read magazine articles about loneliness.

That was when I realised that I was making too many assumptions about God's plan for us. I had to acknowledge once again that God's ways are higher than our ways (Isaiah 55), and that his ways are perfect. It was not for me to dictate the way in which God would be glorified through Roy's illness, nor for me to say when the whole episode was to be over so that I could close the book on it. What I really wanted was for it all to be over so that we could slip back into ordinary, everyday life—and, of course, into all our old ways of taking life, health and all its blessings for granted.

Instead, I still have to trust God for each day as it comes, enjoying each as a precious gift. I have been reminded once again that we have to hold on to God for our daily walk, not just at times of crisis but at all times. And this, in its turn, has made me look closely at my everyday life and whether I am fulfilling God's will for me in the place where he wants me to be.

Apart from my role as wife and supporter to Roy, and mother to a grown-up and increasingly independent family, I also speak regularly to groups of women, telling them the story of how I came to know Jesus. More and more I feel that God is telling me to build them up, those women who come to meetings, often with babies on their laps and toddlers at their knees, and then have to go home to cook meals and clean houses and be the pivot of family life. I feel a great need to affirm women in their role as wives and mothers, because I feel society demands too much of women, and too often demeans them. This is not meant to be a criticism of those who need or want to work: I know that many women have no choice but to be the main or the only breadwinner in their family. But at the same time I also feel sorrow for those who leave tiny children with minders and go out to work either because they are drawn by a desire to have more and more material belongings, or because they feel that they have no value in society's eyes unless they are in paid employment. No one affirms women as homemakers, yet many voices are beginning to be raised in support of the view that society would be improved if more women were available to mother their own children. Ultimately, there can only be a poor substitute for a mother.

Some time ago I spoke at a meeting where I said 'How precious it is before the Lord to be a mother, and do his will.' Afterwards a very worn and tired-looking elderly lady made her way to the front of the hall. As she came up to me I saw that tears were streaming down her face. 'I have a husband and two sons,' she told me, 'and for years I have looked after them and run the home. And no one has ever told me before that what I was doing was worth while.' I couldn't help but think what a crown she will have to wear in heaven, after all her years of selfless work for her family.

At another meeting I addressed a group of women who were all the wives of clergy and other church leaders. Such women have particular stresses in their marriages; their husbands are often on call to large congregations, dealing with crises and problems all the time, and struggling to find time for their own families. Too often the wives feel that the men are doing the really important spiritual work, teaching, evangelising and pastoring other people, and leaving them to run the home and support the work. They may feel resentful or even unimportant. I pointed out to them that if

God spoke to them and said, 'I have a very important task for you. I want you to evangelise two (or three, or four) people. I want you to guide them and teach them and lead them to me, so that I can make leaders and teachers of them in their turn'—well, they would drop everything to go and do such an important job! Yet that is exactly what they have been asked to do, when God entrusted them with the upbringing of their children. They have the chance to shape the environment and structure the world in which their children spend their early years, and the opportunity to show them by their own attitudes and daily life how to walk in God's way and how to know and trust Jesus in their everyday life. Theirs is a vital task.

Yet more women feel that they have to go out to work to earn extra money and improve the family standard of living. So many people sacrifice their time, energy and their relationships to the false gods of material possessions. Fathers work long hours and never see their children, and mothers leave their children with minders and go out to work, not so that they can provide their families with the necessities of food and clothes and shelter, but to keep up with the latest fashions in clothing or furnishings. It is difficult for me to write about these things, because I have been fortunate in my life, and we have seldom been very short of money. Yet I am quite sure that the compulsion to own more and more material possessons of higher and higher quality does not stem from any intrinsic value in the objects, but from a deep need in the personality. If people do not have a sense of self worth, they put their trust in material things as an alternative, as though owning more possessions can prove that they are valuable, successful people.

Roy says that although he came from a very poor family, still, while he was growing up he always felt like a king. His parents made him feel valued for himself, and so he grew up with confidence and self-respect, which no amount of money can buy. Of course, even if we have not been fortunate in the support of our family, and have grown up feeling uncertain and inadequate, there is a sure remedy. There is one person to whom we are always important, who will always love us no matter what, and in whose eyes we have infinite worth. 'God loved the world so much that he gave his only Son so that anyone who believes in him shall not perish but have everlasting life' (John 3:16). Putting our trust in owning material things is pointless, because in the end they are not important, and when we die we must leave them behind. 'Don't store your profits here on earth where they can erode away and be stolen. Store them in heaven where they will never lose their value, and are safe from thieves. If your profits are in heaven, your heart will be there too' (Matthew 6:19–21). The true riches are in knowing God, and if we are doing his will we are 'storing our treasure in heaven'.

I feel that I have peace in my life at the moment, because I am where God wants me to be, doing what he wants me to do. When the children were small I was often too busy for them, trying to work for the church and the community, and getting my priorities all wrong. Fortunately the Lord showed me where I was going wrong, and set my priorities straight. In fact, after I came to know Jesus as my saviour, I found that I was quite content to be at home and concentrate on the needs of the family.

This doesn't mean that I think all women should spend all their time cooking and cleaning and being obsessive about their home—that can become another kind of 'false god' to which people devote their energies. One of the great things I found when I first became a Christian was that God set me free—free to be me. One of the things from which I was set free was the need to have an absolutely immaculate house (yet another attempt to prove myself 'worth while' or 'successful').

I remember that when we first moved into our house at

Gerrards Cross all the carpets were royal blue—we had bought them with the house. When you have dark coloured carpets, one of the first things you find out is that half the dirt in the world is white! They always seemed to be covered in little light-coloured bits of dust and fluff, and they offended my mother terribly. She had always been tremendously well organised when I was a child—she had to be so, to manage her work load of running a home, looking after a family, cleaning the surgery and helping with my father's medical practice. Whenever she came to stay with us, she got me to vacuum those carpets three times a day, because 'You never know who might call, dear.' Her maxim was that first impressions were all-important, and that it really mattered that people should walk into an immaculate hall when they entered the house.

From the early training of my disciplined childhood to her instruction in my early married life, I went on trying to keep everything clean and tidy and well organised. With four children, a husband, and friends and family in and out of a large house, this was rather like painting the Forth Bridge—as soon as the job was finished it was time to start again.

Near the kitchen sink I keep a pad of tear-off sheets, each printed with a Bible verse, which I can change daily. One of these said, 'Study to be quiet' (1 Thessalonians 4:11), and it caused me to argue with God for a long time. 'How can I be quiet, Lord? I have so little time, I'm much too busy, look at all the jobs I have to do.' It took two years—during which I was reminded of that verse, at intervals—before I became obedient, gave in, and asked God to show me how I could do it.

It is fairly unusual for me to be alone in the house during the day (if Roy is not working, he is generally around the house) but that day all was peaceful. I had my lunch, made a cup of tea, sat on the sofa and put my feet up, and asked God to show me where I was going wrong. I realised almost instantly that what drove me to be so busy was a kind of guilt. I could almost hear my mother's voice, saying 'What on earth are you doing sitting there? Look at everything that needs doing!' I realised that all my busyness was a form of trying to please my mother—a way of proving that I was a success as a wife and mother. Yet when we know that God loves us, that he has accepted us, we don't need to prove anything any more. When we are seeking to do his will, we don't have to worry about anything else.

That doesn't mean that we can ignore the demands of the family, though. I remember Daniel coming home from primary school and trying to talk to me while I bustled about the kitchen, cooking supper. 'Mum,' he said patiently, as though suggesting something perfectly obvious to someone unable to see it, 'why couldn't you do the cooking before I came home, so you could play with me now?' He was right, of course, and I saw at once that with a little forethought I could easily make some time to spend with him. It wasn't enough just to be in the same room as him—I had to give him my whole attention at the time when he needed it.

Even when I began to have speaking engagements, once the children were at school, I always made sure that they fitted around Roy and the children, and did not take me away from home when I was needed. This is why I mostly speak to women's groups: all my meetings are day-time ones, so I could always make sure that I was home in time to collect the children from school and be back in my 'mother' role—especially once they were teenagers, when their needs seemed to become more subtle but no less real.

The very fact that I do so much public speaking is an interesting example of the way God has used me, for this is certainly not a natural gift of mine. When I was young, my father was always saying to me, 'Fiona, stop that sentence and say it again without stammering.' I certainly never expected that I would ever be speaking in public!

Some two years after I first became a Christian, a friend rang me and said that her church was holding an 'outreach' coffee morning, and asked whether I would speak at it. I laughed and said, 'No, certainly not!' A few days later she called again, and said, 'Fiona, have you prayed about what I asked you?'

'Yes,' I replied, 'and the answer's still no!'

Pat, however, was nothing if not persistent, and she kept on pestering me. In the end I agreed, but on one condition: that she would share the talk with me, and do it in the form of a question-and-answer session, which we could rehearse beforehand.

Considering I had been on the stage in the West End, it may seem strange that I was so nervous, but I found that it was one thing to act out a role in a musical, and quite another to appear as myself, speaking my own words without a script! I couldn't eat for a week before the coffee morning, and on the day I went down with a cold and a sore throat, so I addressed the meeting of about thirty people in a very croaky voice indeed. However, I got through it. I was just congratulating myself that it was all over, when someone else rang and asked me to do the same thing again!

After a while, another friend encouraged me to dispense with the 'dialogue' double act, and to speak alone—though for a long while I felt I had to write everything down, for fear of losing the thread of what I was saying.

For many years I went on feeling terribly nervous before speaking. When I was driving to an engagement, I would look at other women out shopping and think, 'It's all right for you, you haven't got to go and face a roomful of strangers!' Then one sunny autumn morning on my way to a meeting I saw a young man sweeping up leaves in a park. There is nothing I enjoy so much as sweeping leaves—it's quite my favourite job in the garden—and I thought, 'I'd love to be doing that right now.' And then I suddenly realised that if I were out sweeping leaves I wouldn't be on my way to share the gospel with people, and that was something I really *wanted* to do! It had taken four years, but I had found out how important it was to me that I should share the good news of Christ's love with other people.

Whenever I speak about my early experiences of family life, the tiredness and feeling of being hemmed in by the children, or some of the silly mistakes I made, I can tell by the appreciative laughter from the audience that we are all on the same wavelength: it gives an added dimension to what you say if you can share the everyday experiences of being a wife and mother. So many of the women I speak to have felt the same way, that they take a real interest in the story of how I found meaning and reality in my spiritual life.

When I relate the story of Daniel's accident, and of Roy's illness, I know how closely they are sharing with me in the fears and griefs and joys of those experiences, because they too have husbands and children whom they love dearly. I feel that it is so important that they should be ready to face the ultimate challenge of life—death. If we go through life closing our minds to the possibility of anything bad happening to those we love, then we are living in fear, refusing to face up to reality. Even to watch the television news with its constant stories of war, famine and disaster becomes almost too painful to bear. But if we trust in a loving God, and a Saviour who endured the worst pains the world can offer, even death itself, then we do not need to fear. We know that we and those we love are held safe in God's fatherly love, and that nothing can separate us from that love.

Who then can ever keep Christ's love from us? When we have trouble or calamity, when we are hunted down or destroyed, is it because he doesn't love us any more? And if we are hungry, or penniless, or in danger, or threatened with death, has God deserted us?

No, for the Scriptures tell us that for his sake we must be ready to face death at every moment of the day—we are like sheep awaiting the slaughter.

But despite all this, overwhelming victory is ours through Christ who loved us enough to die for us. For I am convinced that nothing can ever separate us from his love. Death can't, and life can't. The angels won't, and all the powers of hell itself cannot keep God's love away. Our fears for today, our worries about tomorrow, or where we are—high above the sky, or in the deepest ocean—nothing will ever be able to separate us from the love of God demonstrated by our Lord Jesus Christ when he died for us. (Romans 8:35–39, Living Bible)

When my mother was dying, I and my two sisters were looking after her in the granny-annexe built on to my sister's house. After suffering a series of strokes she was severely disabled and bedridden, and the quality of her life had deteriorated. She had said to us, 'I'm ready to go and be with the Lord.' We were deeply sad that she was dying, but we could see that her life was coming to an end, in spite of all the doctor could do. She had always loved music, and on that last evening as we sat with her, I went to switch on her tape recorder. On impulse I put down the orchestral music I had selected, and instead put on a praise tape. The doctor arrived just as we were all three joining in a rousing chorus of 'Shine, Jesus, shine'—it must have sounded as though we were having a party! I invited him in, adding, 'We think Mum's going,' but he said that he would wait in the next room.

'Off you go, Mum—give our love to Jesus!' called Liza. We were singing to her and cheering her on to victory when we suddenly heard the sound of loud nose-blowing from the next room, and we all exploded into giggles. The doctor was surprised and very moved by the thought of Mum being sung on her way into heaven, but we were so sure that she was in Jesus' hands that we didn't have to be gloomy about it.

It is experiences like this in the Christian life which deepen our conviction that everything that happens here on earth is but one part of an ongoing story. I know that death is something to be faced, but not feared. It is the ultimate statistic—one hundred per cent of all people die—and the only sure and predictable event of our life on earth. Yet many people spend their entire lives hiding from the very thought of it, and allow their fear of what may happen to them or their loved ones to colour their whole lives.

Recently a friend commented to me that many people live their life as though it were a dress rehearsal for the real thing. But in fact, by tonight we will have given the only performance of 'today' that we will ever give. So we have to put all our heart, our energy and honesty and sincerity into what we do every day. As a show business family, we find that a very suitable illustration. And every show comes to the end of its run, when we must lay aside the costumes and step off the stage, into another, larger world.

For us as Christians, facing death means facing life, because we know that when we die we follow in the steps of Jesus, who himself rose from death and made possible for us a new life with a renewed and glorious body. And the life we live here on earth meanwhile becomes even more precious and meaningful because it is part of that ongoing life we live in God.

So as we pray the prayer Jesus taught us, we ask God to 'Give us this day'—thankfully receiving one day at a time—looking to him to sustain us with everything we need, whether it be food, shelter, love of family and friends, or courage and hope to face the future. And at the same time we echo the words of the psalmist: 'This is the day the Lord has made. We will rejoice and be glad in it.' (Psalm 118:24).